THE
COTTAGE
garden

THE
COTTAGE
garden

SUE
PHILIPS

conran
OCTOPUS

Project Editor	Jane O'Shea
Project Art Editor	Ann Burnham
Editor	Helen Ridge
Designer	Alistair Plumb
Picture Researcher	Helen Fickling
Editorial Assistant	Caroline Davison
Production	Sonya Sibbons
Illustrators	Shirley Felts
	Gillie Newman
	Valerie Price
	Lesley Craig

CN5614
Typeset by Servis Filmsetting Ltd, England
Printed and bound in Hong Kong

FRONT JACKET Geranium x oxonianum 'Claridge Druce'.

BACK JACKET A typical cottage front garden.

PAGE 1 Borage (Borago officinalis) and honesty (Lunaria annua).

PAGE 2 Nepeta racemosa (syn. N. mussinii), delphiniums and Rosa 'Comte de Chambord'.

RIGHT An informal country cottage garden.

CONTENTS

THE COTTAGE GARDEN TRADITION

Throughout history and all over the world, people living in primitive homes have used their gardens not only to help improve their surroundings but also to raise their standard of living by growing edible, useful or even saleable produce. But the cottage garden style of gardening is regarded as a uniquely British tradition. It is widely thought to be the oldest form of gardening and although it has, over the centuries, developed and moved away from being an aid to subsistence, to many people it is still much more than a hobby – it is a way of life.

The Cottar's Pride – A Cottage Garden
by Henry Sutton Palmer (1854–1933)
This Victorian painting depicts many people's idea of a traditional cottage garden, with the characteristic lack of lawn, overgrown fruit trees and the random nature of the planting, much of which is self-sown.

Cottage gardening as we know it today has its roots in nostalgia, in romantic notions of country life as depicted in Victorian watercolours – the tumble-down cottage, with roses round the door, and rustic damsels tending their hollyhocks surrounded by angelic-looking children. But its history goes back much further than that, and indeed there have been gardens of a sort (or, rather, enclosures) round cottages since medieval times. Throughout the centuries, however, cottage gardens and the way they have been used have changed tremendously – and to some extent they are still changing now.

Cottage garden origins

Medieval cottagers were basically peasants leading a subsistence lifestyle. Their wattle and daub cottages were primitive hovels, consisting of only two rooms, with an open fire in the middle of the larger one, and no chimney to take away the smoke. The 'garden' was not what we would recognize as such today. It was more like a smallholding – an informal yard roughly fenced with hurdles to keep in livestock, who shared the inside of the cottage on winter nights. Feed for the livestock may have been grown in the 'garden', with perhaps a few wild herbs which had been transplanted from the surrounding countryside or a few very basic vegetables, like semi-wild cabbage which was used to flavour the peasants' daily diet of pottage (a thick cereal soup). Only grander establishments like farmhouses had formal gardens for growing vegetables and herbs, and monasteries had positively sophisticated gardens, where the monks cultivated a much wider range of food crops and medicinal herbs.

In Tudor and Elizabethan times, overseas trade brought a wealthy merchant class into being, and exotic new foods, such as figs, almonds and oranges, and spices, such as pepper and ginger, together with foreign styles of cookery and gardening, flooded in from abroad. Money was invested in the land, farmers became wealthy, and villages were improved. But though they may have had better

A Cottage Garden
*by Myles Birket
Foster (1825–99)
This painting shows
the reality behind the
romance: a working
cottage garden as it would
have looked in Victorian
times. All that is missing
is the pigsty, which was to
be found in most cottage
gardens until
comparatively recently.*

LEFT *The earliest cottage
garden plants were useful
rather than just purely
decorative. Today, dual-
purpose plants, as
seen here – the rambler
rose 'Dorothy Perkins',
climbing nasturtiums
(Tropaeolum majus),
creeping thymes,
variegated ajuga, golden
marjoram (Origanum
vulgare 'Aureum') and
sweet woodruff (Asperula
odorata) – are still grown,
even though they may not
be used in the home.*

housing, the peasants who worked on the land were hardly any better off. Their gardens were their larders, and by this time they probably also kept bees for honey, which was used as a sweetening agent since sugar was a scarce and expensive luxury, available only to the rich. Wild flowers may have crept into odd corners too around this time.

Meanwhile, one rung up the social ladder, the wives of small farmers and craftsmen used their gardens to supply all their household requirements: insect repellents, linen deodorizers, medicines and toiletries, as well as flavour enhancers for food and drinks. It was probably they who, trying to keep up with the fashion for ornamental gardening set by the landed gentry, started to grow flowers as well as herbs, vegetables and fruit trees. The gardens of inns must also have looked quite pretty; innkeepers grew herbs such as alecost and clove pinks (*Dianthus caryophyllus*) to flavour the mulled ales and wines that were popular drinks of the day.

The 18th century

By the eighteenth century, another new social class had appeared: the lower middle class, who were tradesmen and artisans. They had gardens round their cottages, which by now were often located in small towns. And, particularly in towns in the north of England, 'florist's societies' began to appear. Florists were not flower sellers as they are today, but amateurs who specialized in growing, breeding and exhibiting particular types of flower. Each society held an annual show at which copper kettles and similar trophies would be presented as prizes; this would be followed by a feast. Indeed, these events were known as 'florist's feasts'. Florists were generally middle-class enthusiasts such as doctors or clergymen, though they might also have been tradesmen and factory workers. In Paisley, Scotland, for instance, the weavers bred pinks and tried to reproduce the intricate patterns of Paisley shawls in the laced patterns on the petals. Pinks (*Dianthus*), auriculas (*Primula auricula*) and ranunculus were among the many 'specialities' they grew, aiming to produce groups with new colours and patterns, and perfectly circular blooms.

In the countryside, important landowners were sufficiently wealthy to move out of their farmhouses close to the village and build themselves mansions on a suitable vantage point, affording good views of the surrounding countryside. They enclosed the land round the house to create a park, and manipulated the landscape to create beautiful views. And since the last thing they wanted was to look out over dilapidated villages, these were frequently demolished. Depending on how humanitarian the landowner was, the peasants were either made homeless, or rehoused in 'model villages' built specially for them. By the late eighteenth century, the fashion for creating picturesque landscapes had developed so far that some villages were designed more to enhance the scenery than to benefit their occupants. Cottages often had a fairy-tale quality about them, with a surfeit of architectural fantasies, such as elaborate chimneys, and virtually no land for the cottager to live off. Some landowners are even said to have paid villagers a wage to walk round dressed as rustic farmhands and milkmaids, to 'decorate' the scene, and impress guests driving up to the park gates.

The 19th century

The ornamental cottages built at the end of the previous century needed gardens to match, and landowners increasingly tried to persuade their tenants to beautify their surroundings. Gardening was fast becoming a fashionable new hobby among the upper echelons of society, and influential gardening writers such as John Claudius Loudon tried to improve the lot of the rural poor by encouraging the gentry to start cottage improvement schemes. Some landowners also introduced competitions with prizes for the best gardens and produce. Around this time rural labourers started to take an interest in gardening proper, and what we now think of as the cottage gardening spirit became manifest, with people passing cuttings over the hedge to neighbours, and sharing out the seeds they had saved. The gardens of the gentry were being enhanced by new and exotic plants, and villagers who worked in these gardens would, clandestinely or otherwise, re-distribute surplus plants or seeds to their friends and relatives.

Cottagers were encouraged to be thrifty and to make the most of what came naturally to improve their gardens. Manure from pigs and poultry was stacked together with garden rubbish and kitchen waste to rot down. Portable earth closets were moved round the garden to enrich the soil, and 'night soil' was also put on the garden. When farm-workers cleared the ditches each year, the fine silt and debris they removed was used to top-dress cottage gardens, rather like mulching today.

Detail of an auricula theatre from the frontispiece of C. Harman Payne's Florist's Bibliography *(1908). This is a reproduction of the original illustration in* Traite de la Culture Parfaite de l'Oreille-d'Ours *(1735) by Sieur de Guenin.*

The Victorian ideal

The romantic cottage gardens we know today – all burgeoning borders with hollyhocks at the gate and roses round the door – did not start appearing until Victorian times. By then, gardening was an absolute obsession for the very wealthy, who sponsored plant-hunting trips abroad, collected exotics such as orchids, and were the first to follow new planting styles, such as carpet bedding. Middle class sub-urban villas sprouted conservatories and geometric borders. The Victorian craze for cottage gardening probably started when water colourists, poets and writers began renovating picturesque old cottages to live in. They planted romantic gardens, evocative of what they saw as the rural idyll, and, for the first time, cottage gardens became decorative rather than purely useful. Given the influx of new foreign plants, all sorts of tender and unusual species soon became part of the cottage garden scene.

The working cottagers, influenced by the horti-cultural changes taking place around them, began

The Farm Garden, Bossington, Somerset *by Arthur Claude Strachan (1865–c.1935)*
Victorian artists had a highly romanticized notion of country life, as this painting of an idyllic cottage garden shows.

growing exotic plants obtained from their new neighbours, and at the same time started using their gardens as a source of income, selling fruit, vegetables and honey. Allotments were started, so those with small gardens could still grow enough to feed their families. Florist's societies began to decline as by this time most craftsmen went away to work long hours in factories, instead of working from home, and had less opportunity to grow and tend their plants. A lot of old varieties of florist's flowers, such as show auriculas (*Primula auricula*), gold- and silver-laced polyanthus, old-fashioned pinks, *Hepatica* and tulips were already being lost, as well as some old cottage flowers which were being replaced by more fashionable kinds.

The Edwardian era

By Edwardian times, herbaceous borders and pergolas had become the latest craze in the fashionable gardens of the wealthy, and, once again, these new ideas filtered down through the social scale. Gardening writers of the time like William Robinson praised the simple cottage garden style, which was also the influence behind the planting schemes of gardeners such as Gertrude Jekyll and Vita Sackville-West, who designed gardens for houses that could never have been considered cottages. Both relied on extravagant colour schemes, Gertrude Jekyll using plants very much as an artist uses paint on a canvas to achieve her effect. However, Vita Sackville-West liked plants to look natural, with climbers growing through each other on walls, self-sown seedlings coming up where they liked, and wild and old-fashioned flowers mixing with the newer exotics. Her garden at Sissinghurst Castle, Kent, still exists and is a prime example of the 'golden age' of cottage gardening. Perhaps because of this and the fact that the garden is a fairly accurate representation of the way it was originally laid out and planted, the 'Sissinghurst style' has probably been the greatest single influence on today's cottage gardeners.

ABOVE *The garden at Sissinghurst Castle in Kent is still maintained very much as it was when originally planted by the writer and gardener Vita Sackville-West. This part of the garden follows a colour scheme of red, orange and yellow, colours often avoided by today's cottage gardeners who often find them difficult to place.*

ABOVE *The author, Sue Phillips, in her cottage garden in West Sussex.*

LEFT *This traditional cottage front garden has a straight path running to the front door through a carpet of plants.*

WHAT IS A COTTAGE GARDEN?

A quick glance is all it takes to identify a cottage garden from any other type of garden. But what makes them so immediately recognizable? Despite their constantly evolving nature and the whims of fashion, most still follow a traditional, unwritten formula – a series of characteristics that, added together, equal 'cottage garden'. Simply blending all the right ingredients, however, will not automatically create a good cottage garden; it still takes a sympathetic spirit on the part of the owner to complete the spell.

A profusion of self-sown flowers, where nature has the upper hand, is the classic formula for a cottage garden. Here, foxgloves (Digitalis purpurea), sweet rocket (Hesperis matronalis), lupins and delphiniums mingle with wild elder bushes (Sambucus nigra) to create the informal look of a rural garden.

Characteristic features

This dense and informal planting, typical of a cottage front garden, is interrupted by a winding, gravel path. The plants – a mixture of colours, sizes, shapes and textures – include lupins (Lupinus), pulmonarias, shasta daisies (Chrysanthemum × superbum), Euphorbia cyparissias, irises and lemon balm (Melissa officinalis).

Rather surprisingly perhaps, a delightful 'olde worlde' cottage is not an essential adjunct of a cottage garden. The cottage garden style of planting is one that can be used to add a touch of rural charm to virtually any small garden whether in town, city or country. What sets a cottage garden apart from other types is its ambience, and that cannot be bought at a garden centre, but has to be painstakingly created by building up traditional elements.

Creating the ambience

Cottage gardens have an air of orderly chaos about them; they look unplanned, overgrown, slightly blowsy even – as if the plants just happened to be there without ever having been planted. They break all the conventional rules of gardening. Plants are often spaced too closely together, and look as if they were shaped by nature instead of secateurs. Tall plants are allowed to flop artistically instead of being held regimentally upright with canes or stakes. Containing, as they do, a lot of fine detail that cannot be taken in at a glance, cottage gardens are best appreciated during a slow, leisurely stroll. In a border, no single highlight stands out from the rest; it is the overall impression that is important. Colours are traditionally bright and randomly mixed, and this sort of colour scheme is now making a comeback after years of muted pastels and limited-spectrum planting schemes being fashionable.

Many old cottage gardens contain an extraordinary blend of formal and informal features that you would expect to clash, but somehow do not. You might, for instance, see a row of standard holly trees (*Ilex aquifolium*), each clipped into a neat lollipop shape, standing out from an undulating hawthorn (*Crataegus. monogyna*) hedge. Or a neat row of scallop shells backed by a straight line of plants which edge a path

ABOVE RIGHT *A meandering path helps lead the eye naturally from one group of plants to the next. The tall shrubs at the back of the borders enclose the area to make a 'garden within a garden'.*

RIGHT *A 'walk-through' planting scheme is filled with lupins (Lupinus), oriental poppies (Papaver orientale), hardy cranesbills (Geranium) and sweet rocket (Hesperis matronalis). The path is nothing more than a single row of paving slabs, barely wide enough for one person.*

background to borders, and they give the garden a longer season of interest. But in the spirit of tradition, many people will choose unusual fruiting plants, such as medlar or quince, and close relatives of native species. Lawns did not feature in traditional cottage gardens either, since lawnmowers were not available and valuable productive space would not have been wasted. Although most of today's cottage gardens have some grass, it is often studded with daisies (*Bellis perennis*) or left slightly rough. In neither case, however, is it a major feature in the way that it is in many other garden styles.

Water can be considered a traditional cottage garden feature. Many original cottage gardens would have had a well or pump to provide water for the house, and very early ones would have had a pond for ducks. Informal or, ideally, slightly 'wild' ponds can therefore be considered appropriate to today's cottage garden. (See also page 60.)

weaving its way through a dense carpet of spreading or self-sown, ground-covering flowers.

Certain types of flower are automatically associated with cottage gardens, especially old-fashioned favourites like hollyhocks (*Alcea rosea*), sweet williams (*Dianthus barbatus*), madonna lilies (*Lilium candidum*) and roses. But today, several other types of plant have crept into the cottage mix, like hybrid lilies (*Lilium*) and large-flowered clematis, even currently fashionable 'collectibles' like euphorbias and alpines, none of which would have figured in traditional cottage gardens. But they now look perfectly at home, and help to add to the garden's colour and interest. Today's cottage gardens are plant-lovers' gardens, laid out as far as possible to re-create the feel of an old garden by keeping within the traditional guidelines, despite the addition of more modern plants or features.

Trees and shrubs, for instance, did not figure very prominently in nineteenth-century cottage gardens, apart from the traditional cottage garden sort — mainly roses and fruit trees and bushes. Today, more trees and shrubs are included in cottage gardens as a

Front gardens

In the earliest cottage gardens, flowers used ornamentally would most likely have been found at the front of the house. This was partly for practical reasons – the front garden was already separated from the livestock, outbuildings, privy, pigsty and cultivated crops kept at the back of the house – but also for aesthetic ones. The front garden was after all permanently on view to the neighbours and passers-by, and if a landlord wanted to create a pretty show village for his own benefit, then it was the front garden he would particularly have encouraged tenants to 'decorate' accordingly. The layout of a front garden depended very much on the shape of the plot on which the cottage was built; this would often have been very irregular, though several traditional plans emerged. A range of planting styles, varying from strictly formal to totally wild, also existed.

Formal and informal styles

Victorian watercolours show cottages with front gardens so informal they could only have been the result of self-seeding and a generous measure of neglect. They may have had no front garden at all, with the cottage fronting straight on to a lane with clumps of hollyhocks (*Alcea rosea*), valerian (*Valeriana officinalis*), primroses (*Primula vulgaris*) or other flowers tucked into odd corners, or there may have been a hedge and a patch of rough grass, with perhaps an apple tree and flowers growing at random. Being romantics, however, Victorian artists tended to prefer very tumbledown cottages as a subject, so the gardens they painted were probably not entirely typical. Cottage gardens belonging to artisans and professional people were better tended, and were informally styled, aiming at generous abundance, rather than a neglected style.

Early twentieth-century cottage front gardens again fell into two camps, as can be seen from illustrations and early black and white photographs of the time. Small cottages had front gardens which appeared to be overwhelmingly formal, with a straight path running to the front door and a carpet of flowers growing on either side of it. These often had several formal rows of flowers along the edge of

the path, perhaps with a line of sea shells in front of them, and an informal mixture of flowers behind. If there was not much back garden, rows of vegetables would be tucked in behind the flowers in the front garden. Some terraced cottages had gardens that consisted almost entirely of different rows of flowers planted parallel with the path, and this would be all that divided the garden from next door's path and their rows of flowers.

Some larger cottages, whose owners were wealthier, had front gardens with perhaps a patch of lawn surrounded by abundantly planted cottage borders, and winding paths leading to the back of the house. Or the owner may have chosen a very natural look, with the front garden filled completely with a profusion of flowers. There were, of course, no cars, garages, or drives to be incorporated then, so it is probably inevitable that today's cottage front garden will look slightly different from its nineteenth-century counterpart.

ABOVE *Well-stocked perennial borders line the path to this cottage front door.*

ABOVE RIGHT *A vegetable patch is tucked in behind an edging of flowers in which gladioli, zinnias and cornflowers (*Centaurea cyanus) *predominate.*

RIGHT *Even the tiniest front garden has room for a welcoming display of climbers such as roses and everlasting pea (*Lathyrus latifolius)*, accompanied here by foxgloves.*

Since historical information provides such a choice of authentic front garden styles, it is not difficult to find something among them that can be adapted to suit today's cottage gardens. Nowadays a very popular small cottage front garden may consist of gravel paths running between cottage beds and borders, with small plants permitted to seed themselves into the gravel to soften the outlines. A garden like this often starts from a more 'conventional' layout – a small lawn containing cottagey beds or borders. In time, as beds are enlarged to accommodate an increasing collection of plants, all that is left of the lawn is a series of grass paths which become muddy from over-use in wet weather, until eventually the owner strips off what is left of the turf and replaces it with gravel. Although it sounds deceptively simple, it is typical of the natural evolution of cottage gardens – and you might be surprised to discover how many of the most successful of today's cottage gardens 'happened' in this way.

provided some food for the household. Today a mixed hedge is invaluable for providing shelter on an exposed site, allowing you to grow more difficult, delicate plants inside the garden. It also forms a good leafy backdrop to your borders. A hedge of thorny species like eglantine (*Rosa rubiginosa*, syn. *R. eglanteria*) and hawthorn (*Crataegus monogyna*) can add considerably to the security of the garden.

In areas where stone was quarried locally, stone boundary walls were built round cottage gardens and they can still be seen today. Where there was plenty of coppiced woodland to supply the raw materials, sheep hurdles may have been used as the earliest garden boundaries. Hurdles are also handy for plugging a gap in a hedge, even if you do not want to make an entire fence from them. But as a general rule, any natural material that is available locally, in good supply and cheaply, can be considered a suitable material for creating a cottage garden boundary. It is, after all, what a traditional cottager would have used.

Compartments within the garden

Odd-shaped plots lend themselves naturally to being divided into smaller 'gardens within gardens'. But internal partitions may be added to any garden (see Regular and irregular plots on page 50). The garden can be divided up using bold groups of tall plants, formal hedges, rustic fencing, climbers or trained cane fruit on post-and-wire supports, or even just flower borders, paths or open space. Creating partitions is a very successful way of getting a lot of detail into even a relatively small garden, while keeping it reasonably well structured. By using this technique you can create small 'theme' areas within the main garden, each of which is almost like a miniature garden in its own right. These not only make a garden more interesting to walk round, they also give you scope to have fun exploring separate design concepts, trying out all sorts of planting combinations and new ideas without worrying that a mistake would affect your pleasure in the rest of the garden. You might choose to have a herb garden (see page 30), a chamomile lawn (see page 31), an ornamental vegetable garden (see page 68), or a paved garden with lots of pots (see page 64).

A low, stone wall makes a natural division between two entirely different styles of planting without creating a lot of shade. A formal row of bearded irises is planted in front of the wall with an underplanting of stonecrop (Sedum acre) softening the hard edge of the gravel path.

Shaping the garden

Lacking the lawn or large areas of paving that define the basic shape of a modern garden, the cottage garden relies on several rather less prominent features to fulfil the same role. The outer boundary of the garden, internal dividers and paths all help to underline the various shapes involved. Such features help to add detail to the garden but, more important still, they add detail at different heights to the main attraction – the flower borders.

Garden boundaries

Most traditional cottage gardens would have been surrounded by a typically rural, mixed boundary hedge of wild and fruiting trees which acted as a defence against neighbouring livestock and also

Edging to beds

A common feature of traditional cottage gardens was the use of edging materials to outline paths and flower beds. This helped to give shape to a garden that consisted of little more than a carpet of plants. In a modern garden, it has a practical purpose too, since hard edging stops gravel running from a path into adjacent flower beds.

Traditional edgings include low-growing plants like daisies (*Bellis perennis*), london pride (*Saxifraga umbrosa*), mounds of houseleeks (*Sempervivum* species) or pinks (*Dianthus*), or solid objects like a row of scallop shells or bricks laid corners-up to make a zigzag pattern. A warning about shells, however: even if you can eat enough shellfish to make a border to a path, the shells are awkward to use as they keep falling over, and weeding between them is a night-

mare. A traditional path edging would often be made up of several rows, so you might have a line of bricks with one or two rows of flowers behind it.

The attractive Victorian twist-topped terracotta edging tiles were commonly used for edging cottage garden paths and modern-day reproductions of these, though enormously expensive, have made them popular once again. They are available in a charcoal shade as well as the usual clay colour. You may even be lucky enough to find second-hand original edging tiles in architectural salvage yards. Terracotta floor tiles, laid cornerwise to give a jagged edge, are much used in today's cottage gardens. Also enjoying a revival are very neat, low, clipped hedges of lavender (*Lavandula* species) or dwarf box (*Buxus sempervirens* 'Suffruticosa'), a feature borrowed from knot gardens and parterres of the past.

*A trimmed box hedge outlines a garden set within a garden. Inside, a rather exuberant mass of tall vatican sage (*Salvia sclarea turkestanica*), perovskia and penstemons in soft pink-mauves and silvery shades contrasts with the formality and more vivid colours of Sedum spectabile, achilleas and penstemons in the late summer border outside.*

Rustic features

Cottage gardens do not rely solely on plants for their effect; 'hard' rustic features, such as arches and arbours, are important as well to provide a contrast in colour and texture to all the flowers. Seats, gravel or brick paths (see page 49), as well as ornaments like bird tables, are also used to add rural character to a garden. Strategically placed, they are a good way of creating contrast within a sea of plants, helping to create focal points that visually break up the scenery into areas the eye can take in at a glance. Suitably rustic features also help create the right atmosphere in the garden. But they must never dominate. Understatement is the secret of success. Everything should look weathered, as though it just grew up spontaneously with the garden, rather than being deliberately chosen and placed.

Arches

Arches are a good feature for linking different parts of the garden, making it obvious to anyone walking round that a slight change of scene lies ahead. They also introduce height into the garden, and enable you to grow climbing plants you might not otherwise have room for. Arches can be bought ready-made from sawn timber with trellis-covered sides, but far more appropriate to the cottage garden are the ones you make yourself from rustic poles, using criss-crossed pieces of branch over the top and sides.

Climbing plants All sorts of climbing plants can be trained over an arch, but a mixture of roses, clematis and honeysuckle (*Lonicera*) looks both traditional and pretty. Annual climbers, such as sweet peas (*Lathyrus odoratus*) or morning glory (*Ipomoea purpurea*), are useful to cover the base of tall, woody stemmed climbers like roses, or simply to add extra flower interest, particularly to a newly planted arch. Or, as a change, climbing fruit such as blackberries look cottagey, besides solving a common problem – that of fitting everything in.

When starting off a climber, plant it 30–45cm (1–1½ft) away from the base of the support, as the support itself will tend to deflect rainwater, leaving a dry area round its base. Dig in plenty of organic matter before planting, and lead the climber up on to the support by pushing an inclined cane into the ground alongside it, securing the top firmly against the support. Tie the first new shoots in place, even in the case of self-twining climbers, until they start to get a grip for themselves.

This rose arch of copper-pink 'Albertine', a popular cottage garden rambler, sets off the view to perfection. Geranium endressii 'Wargrave Pink' and G. 'Johnson's Blue', Senecio bicolor cineraria 'White Diamond' and Argyranthemum frutescens complete the setting.

CLIMBING PLANTS
Perennial climbers
Clematis species
  and hybrids
Climbing rose
Everlasting pea
  (*Lathyrus latifolius*)
Grape vine
  (*Vitis vinifera*)
Honeysuckle (*Lonicera*)
Hops (*Humulus lupulus*)
Summer jasmine
  (*Jasminum officinale*)
Winter jasmine
  (*Jasminum nudiflorum*)

Annual climbers
Asarina barclayana
Canary creeper
  (*Tropaeolum peregrinum*)
Climbing nasturtium
  (*Tropaeolum majus*)
Cup and saucer plant
  (*Cobaea scandens*)
Morning glory
  (*Ipomoea purpurea*)
Purple bell vine
  (*Rhodochiton
  atrosanguineus*)
Sweet pea
  (*Lathyrus odoratus*)

Garden seats

Pretty bench seats, strategically situated at the end of a walk, or in a niche in the hedge, provide a focal point in themselves and turn a group of plants into one of the garden's beauty spots. Because they are an important part of the scenery, it is essential to choose seats that can be left out all year – hardwood or cast aluminium are the best materials unless you can run to genuine Victorian cast iron. You can also buy or make hardwood seats that fit round the trunks of trees; they look particularly effective round the old gnarled apple tree every cottage garden should have. Wirework chairs have an authentic look; you can sit on them, but they look far better overgrown with climbers and surrounded by plants in pots.

Arbours and bowers

If you put an arch and a seat together, you have created an arbour or bower. Technically, an arbour is defined as having the sides and roof made of rustic poles or trelliswork upon which plants climb, while a bower is formed by walls of leafy plants. Both were regular features of traditional cottage gardens.

It is not difficult to construct your own arbour by making a timber framework supporting trellis on the sides, back and roof, though a more truly cottage version would be made of rustic poles and criss-crossed branches. Alternatively, tall, preferably ever-green, hedges can be planted round three sides of a seat to make a bower, with pergola poles above forming the roof on which climbers can be grown. Traditionally, scented climbing plants like roses and honeysuckle (*Lonicera*) were grown over a bower, but you could also plant herbs and scented-leaved pelar-goniums round it. Flowers that are most heavily perfumed after dusk, such as night-scented stock (*Matthiola bicornis*) and sweet rocket (*Hesperis matro-nalis*), are the most suitable choice for people who enjoy sitting in the garden in the evenings.

Climbing roses, especially well-scented ones, are ideal arbour plants. Three plants will give a good cover for this size of arbour, and by using the same cultivar such as the 'Leverkusen' illustrated here, you will have a more dramatic display.

Seats are more than just somewhere to sit – they form part of the scenery in a cottage garden. Hardwood or metal seats which can be left out all year are the most practical. In a wild part of the garden, a rustic seat can be almost overwhelmed by vegetation. Here, self-sown aquilegias, welsh poppies (Meconopsis cambrica) and foxgloves (Digitalis) flourish in an informal display, with wild cow parsley (Antriscus sylvestris) in the hedgerow behind.

23

The style of planting

Self-seeders and spreaders are left to fend for themselves in this front garden. The secret of success is to have a wide variety of plant shapes for contrast. Here, verbascums, golden rod (Solidago), Allium giganteum, Calendula officinalis and evening primrose (Oenothera biennis) fill the centre of the plot, with dahlias, phlox and sunflowers forming an irregular boundary.

Cottage gardens are characterized by their disorderly appearance, which makes them look as though they were never actually planned and planted, but just evolved naturally. In the earliest cottage gardens, this effect was usually achieved in exactly that way.

Spreaders and self-seeders

By letting loose a mixture of rampant spreading plants and self-seeders into the beds (especially those in front gardens which were most likely to be a solid carpet of plants), and letting them fight it out among themselves, the cottager managed to create a very low-maintenance garden. All available ground space would have been densely covered from spring to autumn, and weeds would not have stood a chance against the rising tide of foliage.

Gardens of this type are still seen today (see the planting plan on pages 42–3). This style of planting is a useful way of filling a border that is required to look mature in a hurry, or if lack of time means you want a cottage garden that can largely be left to take care of itself. The only real work involved, beyond mulching in spring and clearing debris in autumn, is pulling out any plants that come up where you do not want them. But low-maintenance cottage borders only 'work' if the soil is completely free of perennial weeds from the start (see page 40). After three to five years, you can expect such a border to become badly congested. Then it is time to remove and split all the plants in autumn or early spring (see page 97), improve the soil by digging in lots of well-rotted organic matter (see page 36), and replant the young, healthy divisions.

RAMPANT SPREADERS
Achillea ptarmica 'The Pearl'
Ajuga reptans cultivars
Bluebells (*Hyacinthoides non-scripta*)
Campanula glomerata
Campanula portenschlagiana
Comfrey (*Symphytum grandiflorum*)
Fox and cubs (*Hieracium aurantiacum*)
Geranium procurrens
Golden rod (*Solidago* hybrids)
Japanese anemone (*A. japonica* cultivars)
Maltese cross (*Lychnis chalcedonica*)
Mint (*Mentha* species)
Snow in summer (*Cerastium tomentosum*)
Tansy (*Tanacetum vulgare*)

Geranium sylvaticum 'Album' and golden feverfew (Tanacteum parthenium 'Aureum') make a cool and simple composition of ground cover plants for light shade.

'Walk-through' borders

You could create a complete 'walk-through' planting scheme, with clumps of tall plants such as *Euphorbia characias wulfenii* and evening primrose (*Oenothera biennis*) standing out from a sea of low ground-covering plants, such as lady's mantle (*Alchemilla mollis*) and bugle (*Ajuga*), with winding gravel paths or just odd paving stones to help you pick your way through. To make the most of a walk-through border, dot self-seeding hardy annuals like field poppies (*Papaver rhoeas*) and nasturtiums (*Tropaeolum majus*) between the plants in spring, to give attractive splashes of colour in summer. After the first year they should seed themselves, and all you need do is remove those that come up too thickly or where you do not want them. I find a few clumps of annuals dotted about in this sort of border look better than a complete carpet of flowers.

Special plants

Useful though these low-maintenance schemes undoubtedly are, they would not suit most people as a means of filling the entire garden. Today's cottage gardeners are often plant enthusiasts who see a garden as the ideal place in which to grow many different plants requiring specialist attention. He or she invariably grows a lot of choice small treasures like auriculas (*Primula auricula*), gold- and silver-laced polyanthus, old named varieties of primrose, old-fashioned pinks, violets and violas (see page 92). It is essential to keep these choice plants in separate beds, well away from aggressive smotherers. This enables you, as well, to give them the precise conditions in which they thrive. They can then be teamed with plants that set them off nicely, require the same sort of growing conditions and do not prove a threat to their well-being.

Achieving a balance

The vast majority of plants grown in today's cottage gardens lies somewhere in between the two extremes in terms of size and rampant tendencies, and these can quite safely be grown together without mishap. The great trick is knowing which are which. Plants that are perfectly docile for one person can, on a different soil type, go berserk – for example, lady's mantle. Finding out how individual plants perform is all part of the fun of cottage gardening.

Traditional cottage plants

Old-fashioned and species roses – Rosa rugosa *'Fru Dagmar Hastrup'*, R. glauca *and* R. gallica *'Versicolor' – and woodbine (*Lonicera periclymenum*), yellow loosestrife (*Lysimachia punctata*), Nepeta racemosa, Geranium endressii *'Wargrave Pink'*, Senecio *'Sunshine' and hebes (not yet in flower) are planted in a traditional, random mixture of colours and shapes.*

Certain types of plant are traditionally associated with cottage gardens, especially wild flowers, herbs, old-fashioned flowers and the more specialist collector's plants. And although you may choose to include some more modern cultivars, as well as many plants that would never have been grown in the past, at least by including a good selection of reasonably authentic plants and flowers, you will end up with a garden that is recognizably cottagey in style.

Old-fashioned flowers

Which are the old-fashioned flowers? There are no hard and fast rules, but for most people the term covers a wide mixture of plants, including non-culinary herbs, such as those used for medicinal purposes (see page 98), flowers derived from wild ancestors, the major and minor florist's flowers (see right) and, of course, the old roses.

Old-fashioned plants include many Victorian cottage garden favourites, a number of which were almost lost from cultivation when gardening fashions changed at the end of Queen Victoria's reign. Even plants bred earlier this century are now being collected again by enthusiasts as old-fashioned flowers. These include Russell lupins (*Lupinus*), raised by George Russell, and many cultivars of violet and viola such as *Viola* 'Jackanapes' and 'Bowles Black'. Many old-fashioned flowers were almost lost in the 1960s and 1970s when low-maintenance gardens of shrubs and ground cover plants were in vogue and several older cultivars of flowering plants were dropped by the nursery trade in favour of 'better' new varieties. However, old-fashioned flowers and cottage garden plants, which still form the basis of the authentic cottage garden style of planting, are now back in favour and can easily be found in specialist nurseries.

TRADITIONAL COTTAGE FLOWERS
Crown imperials
  (*Fritillaria imperialis*)
Daisies (*Bellis perennis*)
Hollyhocks (*Alcea rosea*)
London pride
  (*Saxifraga umbrosa*)
Madonna lilies
  (*Lilium candidum*)
Pinks (*Dianthus*)
Primroses
  (*Primula vulgaris*)
Roses (*Rosa*)
Sunflowers (*Helianthus*)
Sweet williams
  (*Dianthus barbatus*)
Violets (*Viola*)

Roses

For enthusiasts, the beauty of old-fashioned roses is their scent, which often out-performs that of the best Hybrid Teas. Equally enticing are their shapes, rarely found in modern roses. Some have 'quartered' flowers, which are flattish and look as if they have been sliced in four with a knife. Others, such as *Rosa* 'Fantin-Latour', have flowers like the buttons on Victorian sofas, while those of 'Chapeau de Napoléon' are a cocked-hat shape. Moss roses, such as 'Old Pink Moss', have buds and stem tips covered in what look like mossy outgrowths, and the cabbage rose (*R. × centifolia*) has large, loose, blowsy flowers resembling those in paintings by the Dutch Masters.

Even the colour range of old roses is different. There are few strident oranges or vivid reds, but a lot of soft, smoky purples like that of *R.* 'Cardinal de Richelieu'. Particularly lovely are the flowers that change colour as they open and mature – one of my favourites is 'William Lobb' – and also those with striped petals such as *R.* 'Camaieux'. (See also page 93 and the planting plan on pages 94–5).

Collector's plants

Part of the fun of cottage gardening lies in searching out interesting, choice and unusual old cottage garden plants from remote nurseries or at plant fairs. Very often collectormania strikes, and people become interested in growing one type of plant that particularly appeals to them – perhaps campanulas, old roses, or primroses. As a cottage garden relies on a variety of plant detail for its effect, it is probably the only style of garden that can absorb a special interest such as this and still look like a garden rather than a botanical collection.

Florist's flowers

The different types of plant in which the florists specialized became known as florist's flowers (see page 9), and the earliest of these were auriculas, carnations (*Dianthus* hybrids), tulips, anemones and ranunculus; double hyacinths (*Hyacinthus orientalis*),

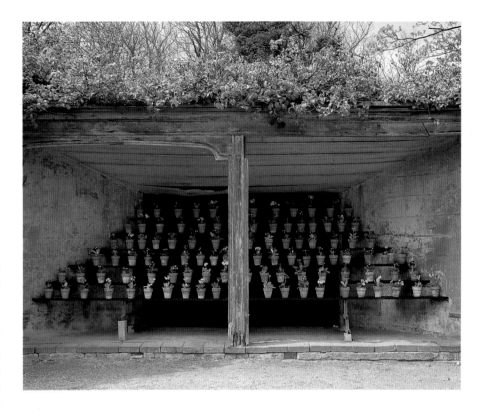

gold- and silver-laced polyanthus and pinks were added to the list somewhat later. At the height of their popularity, there were hundreds of different named varieties of any one florist's flower. But often there was little difference between cultivars, because any grower could produce thousands of seedlings and call them what he liked, and very often another grower would have bred something very similar under a different name. Nowadays, the relatively few old varieties of florist's flower that still remain, as well as new varieties currently being bred, make up a growing group of collector's plants that are much sought after by cottage gardeners.

As well as the ten or so oldest and best known florist's flowers, plant enthusiasts of the past grew and bred other, easier flowers to a lesser extent. These 'second string' florist's flowers included pansies and violets (*Viola*), primroses (*Primula vulgaris*), hepatica, wallflowers (*Cheiranthus*), pelargoniums, penstemons, hollyhocks (*Alcea rosea*), sweet rocket (*Hesperis matronalis*), sweet williams (*Dianthus barbatus*), roses, fuchsias, cottage chrysanthemums (*Dendranthema rubellum*) and dahlias.

An auricula theatre in an enthusiast's garden displays a collection of self-coloured, grey-edged and green show auriculas (Primula auricula) growing in clay flower pots. The structure is north-facing to provide cool shady conditions, and the roof prevents the delicate farina on the leaves and the paste on the flowers from becoming marked.

Show auriculas Being small and easy to grow in pots, auriculas made ideal florist's flowers. Due to the powdery coating on the leaves and the 'paste' on the flowers, the plants had to be cultivated under a glass cover to prevent rain spoiling them. Originally they were grown under industrial glass chemical jars with the bottoms removed, but later they were cultivated under bell-jars. The plants were often dramatically displayed in auricula 'theatres', which had tiers of shelves and velvet drapes. Even today, to see auriculas at their best when in flower, you should display them in pots on shelves, in a shady, sheltered part of the garden.

Like showmen of today, the old auricula exhibitors each had their special secrets for producing prize-winning specimens. Heavy manuring and annual repotting was considered necessary for producing large flowers. One expert top-dressed his plants with a mixture of sheep's blood and poultry manure mixed with potting compost; another swore by a compost mixture containing bullock's blood, 'night soil' and sugar scum. Today, auriculas are still shown by enthusiasts, grown in well-ventilated and shaded cold frames, using a proprietary soil-based compost, perhaps with a little grit and leafmould or coco-fibre added. In summer, the frame lids should be raised to allow in plenty of fresh air. Show auriculas are martyrs to soil pests, especially root aphids and vine weevils (see page 40).

Wild plants

Looking through a book on wild flowers, it is quite amazing to see how many of them, albeit ones that are no longer very common in the wild, are traditional cottage garden flowers. Plants like fox and cubs (*Hieracium aurantiacum*), primroses (*Primula vulgaris*), cowslips (*Primula veris*) and dusky cranesbills (*Geranium phaeum*) are just a few. Early cottagers would have simply dug up the more colourful wild flowers from the countryside (illegal nowadays) and tucked them into an odd spot in the garden.

Untypical forms, such as those with unusual colours, larger flowers than normal or perhaps double flowers, would have been particularly desirable. Left in the wild, these 'sports' may not have survived; double flowers do not normally set seed, and any freak is usually less robust than the normal form. But once safely established in a cottage garden, these curiosities selected from among the local wild flowers would have had a chance to thrive, and may in time have been passed over the garden fence to neighbours who admired them. In this way particular variants would have become common locally and in a gradual way joined the ranks of cottage flowers.

Cross-pollination

A certain amount of cross-pollinating must have taken place in the old gardens, and since it was usual

*Meadow buttercup (*Ranunculus acris*) and Bachelor's buttons (*Ranunculus acris* 'Flore Pleno')*

*Lesser celandine (*Ranunculus ficaria*) and* Ranunculus ficaria *'Brazen Hussy'*

*Honesty (*Lunaria annua*) and Variegated honesty (*Lunaria annua variegata*).*

Wild flowers should be kept to their own part of the garden, as some may seed excessively and swamp more treasured plants. Here, heartsease (Viola tricolor), mayweed (Matricaria chamomilla) and white campion (Silene alba) have been planted against a backdrop of red campion (Silene dioica), honesty (Lunaria annua) and mullein (Verbascum), with buddleja which will attract butterflies.

LEFT *Original wild flowers and their cultivated counterparts found in cottage gardens today are illustrated here (not to scale) in pairs.*

to let plants self-seed, new cultivars must have arisen spontaneously within the gardens themselves. Particularly pretty forms would have been further encouraged to proliferate, and eventually passed around. In time, some cultivars were deliberately bred, using wild stock or its direct descendants as the original parents. Today, there are a huge number of cottage garden flowers that are the second cousins of wild flowers. A few familiar ones can be traced back to sports found in the wild, such as the double-flowered bachelor's buttons known as *Ranunculus acris* 'Flore Pleno'. More recent finds are being added to the roll-call all the time, and one of the most recent discoveries is the very attractive, bronze-leaved form of celandine, now named *Ranunculus ficaria* 'Brazen Hussy', discovered by Christopher Lloyd, the well-known contemporary gardening writer, in woods near his home.

Growing wild plants

Cottage garden plants that are derived from wild flowers are generally less vigorous or tough than their wild parents, and they need cultivating rather than being left to fend for themselves. This is especially true of some of the choicer types; old primrose cultivars, for instance, are particularly difficult to keep alive, let alone grow well. But for some people, the challenge is all part of the fun of growing them.

Wild flowers and their cultivated close relatives do best in soil which has not been treated with fertilizers, either artificial or organic. The soil should be prepared by digging in plenty of organic matter. Choose planting positions that most closely duplicate the conditions in which the plant grows in the wild. For instance, purple loosestrife (*Lythrum salicaria*), celandines (*Ranunculus ficaria cupreus*) and lady's mantle (*Alchemilla mollis*) enjoy wet, heavy soil; primroses (*Primula vulgaris*), wood anemones (*Anemone nemorosa*) and violets (*Viola*) prefer moist shade and shelter under trees, and soil containing lots of leafmould; cowslips (*Primula veris*) do better given a more open, sunny situation growing in grass, while most cranesbills (*Geranium* species) and mallow (*Malva* species) enjoy a basically sunny spot in the company of roses or other shrubs that provide light shade for part of the day.

Herbs

Along with vegetables and fodder for livestock, herbs were almost certainly the first plants to be grown in cottage gardens. From the time early cottagers started making any sort of garden round their homes, they would have grown herbs, though not for purely culinary use. Herbs were the raw materials used then to make just about everything you needed to run a medieval household – herbal remedies, toiletries, household products such as insect repellents, air freshener, linen perfumes, and dyes for wool, as well as flavourings for food and drinks such as mulled ales and wines (see pages 98–9 for a descriptive list of such plants). The word herb actually meant useful plant, and even though you may not want to use them for their original purpose, the non-culinary sort of herbs are appropriate plants to grow in a cottage garden today, along with the usual culinary species, many of which will be found in the planting plan on pages 72–3.

Mixing herbs with flowers

In a border, herbs blend well with flowers. Many have attractive coloured foliage, which makes an effective contrast with adjacent flowering plants; others have aromatic foliage and are good for growing along the edge of a path where you will brush past them, releasing their scent. Low-growing herbs like creeping thyme (*Thymus* species) can be grown in the cracks between paving to scent the air as you walk over them.

Self-contained herb gardens

Since herbs have again become fashionable, many people nowadays like to create a separate herb garden, which need not be large – a bed two metres (six feet) square would be sufficient. Herb gardens traditionally have a fairly formal layout (see the planting plan on pages 72–3), with gravel or brick paths separating the beds, and an ornament such as a bird bath or sundial or a specimen plant in a large terracotta pot in the centre. The use of 'hard' materials sets off the surrounding foliage; without them, a herb garden is in danger of looking like a sea of unbroken green.

The edge of the garden can be outlined formally with clipped hedges of dwarf box or lavender, or informally with low plants like golden marjoram (*Origanum vulgare* 'Aureum') spilling out over the paths. Alternatively you could simply use a row of twist-topped terracotta tiles to mark the outer boundary of the garden. These could also be used inside the garden to edge beds, though on a small scale it makes better use of space to plant rows of those herbs you use a lot, such as parsley (*Petroselinum crispum*) or chives (*Allium schoenoprasum*), as edgings.

The key to growing any herbs is a warm, sunny spot, reasonably well sheltered from wind, with free-draining soil. If you do not have this naturally, beds can be raised up slightly, and surrounded by a low wall of old bricks, stone blocks or timber, and coarse grit forked into the soil to provide extra drainage. Surrounding walls and hard paths all help to reflect heat and provide the right sort of environment for herbs to do well.

Since relatively few herbs are very colourful, it is worth including some specially for their flowers, like nasturtium and borage (*Borago officinalis*), and letting chives flower instead of cutting them back as you normally would. You could also include coloured

Traditional herb gardens are often very formal and geometrically shaped, but in a cottage garden setting an altogether softer approach can be more appropriate. In this garden, stepping stones run through a carpet of creeping thymes, and culinary herbs are joined by the far wider range of herbs that cottagers of old would have used to supply many of their household needs. The tall purplish red plant is red orache (Atriplex hortensis 'Rubra'); the plant with umbels of white flowers, resembling cow parsley, is sweet cicely (Myrrhis odorata).

Chamomile lawns would not have featured in old cottage gardens, but they are typical of the gradual changes that have crept into cottage gardening over the centuries. They are reputed to be difficult to grow, but given very good drainage, they thrive. Here, non-flowering Chamaemelum nobile 'Treneague' has been planted through a layer of gravel to assist drainage.

Rosmarinus officinalis **(Rosemary)**
'Rosemary for remembrance' forms the basis of many old traditions. Garlands of the herb were carried by brides, used to decorate churches and halls for festivals and other special occasions, and thrown into graves by mourning relatives. Rosemary had all sorts of medicinal and household functions, too. It was widely used in hair tonics and rinses to promote hair growth; fresh sprigs were added to the hot coals in warming pans to perfume the sheets, while the stems were said to clean and whiten the teeth. As its scent was thought to have anti-infective properties, rosemary was often burnt in sick-rooms.

leaved herbs such as purple sage (*Salvia officinalis* 'Purpurascens') or tricolour sage (*S. officinalis* 'Tricolor') and purple basil (*Ocimum basilicum* 'Dark Opal').

Herb lawns

Herb lawns would probably not have featured in nineteenth-century cottage gardens, but they do have the right ambience for a modern one. The site for a herb lawn must be very well drained and in full sun; improve the soil by digging in grit as well as organic matter, and then spread a 5cm (2in) layer of gravel, through which the herbs are planted. On less than perfectly drained soil, it is best to dig in enough grit to raise the lawn area up by several centimetres and make a low retaining wall round the edge to ensure adequate drainage.

The plant usually grown for herb lawns is the non-flowering form of chamomile (*Chamaemelum nobile* 'Treneague'), which is sold as cuttings by herb specialists; the flowering form looks straggly when coming into flower, though it can be used if you do not mind cutting it more often. Alternatively, creeping thyme can be used. Avoid walking on a herb lawn too much; to cut it, trim it with shears, and remove any weeds by hand.

Pot-grown herbs

Herbs make good subjects for containers too (see also page 64) and look best grown in terracotta pots. Whether you intend to plant the herbs out eventually, or to keep them in their pots, a good collection can be housed by the back door, or positioned up some steps. Choose plants for a good range of height, shape, texture and scent; grow them in pots of different sizes and include a few pots with raised patterns or elaborate shapes to add interest to a collection. Try teaming an upright rosemary (*Rosmarinus officinalis*), tricolour sage (*Salvia officinalis* 'Tricolor'), french lavender (*Lavandula stoechas*), thyme (*Thymus vulgaris*), and greek oregano (*Origanum* species) for a group that looks and smells lovely, but is also useful in cooking. Bush basil (*Ocimum basilicum*) makes a neat rounded bush, good for growing as a specimen plant in a large terracotta pot by the back door; it is said to keep flies out of the house. Very vigorous, spreading herbs, like comfrey (*Symphytum officinale*), russian tarragon (*Artemisia dracunculoides*), mint (*Mentha* species) and tansy (*Tanacetum vulgare*) are best planted in large flower pots to keep their roots confined; these can then be plunged up to the rim in a bed or border.

Village life

In the past, rural communities were invariably isolated and impoverished. In the days before sophisticated shops and consumer goods, radio and television, and private or public transport, the village was a close-knit community that relied on its own resources, and cottage gardening played an essential role in everyday village life.

Self-sufficiency

Villagers passed plants around among themselves, saved their own vegetable seeds, stored fruit and root crops for winter, dried herbs and made preserves and home-made wine. They also kept bees for honey and to make mead, and improved their garden soil by using whatever came naturally (see page 10). Bowers and arches were made from fallen branches, and slates or stone blocks from old cottages were retrieved and used round the garden. Cottagers also made their own baskets, gates, fences and indoor furniture. Today, few real cottage gardeners will buy what they can grow or make for themselves. They propagate their own plants and swap seeds with friends, as well as learning woodland crafts and other old country skills, which are now making a comeback. These can be used to good decorative and productive effect in a rural garden.

Joining societies

Specialist plant and gardening societies always strike me as a natural extension of the old cottage gardening 'plant share' philosophy. If you are a keen propagator, it is specially well worth joining a plant society as this way you have access to a lot of unusual seeds and plants at very low cost (see page 96). At meetings there is often a bring-and-buy plant stall, and occasionally plant sales are arranged, to which far-flung nurseries are invited. Several societies have a seed distribution scheme for members; the idea is

Cottage gardens traditionally had flowers growing in the front garden and vegetables in the back. This row of rural cottages, with a vegetable plot of cabbages and runner beans, seems to have changed little from those cottage gardens painted by the Victorians a century ago.

that if you save and contribute seed from your own plants, you are then entitled to receive a larger 'share' than non-contributing members.

Local gardening clubs are one of the last strongholds of village community life, and they are a good way of meeting people with whom you can swap cuttings, or find out about local sources of farmyard manure, rustic poles, and other essential gardening requirements. Some clubs offer members a discount at local garden centres, or run their own sundries or seed sales at knock-down prices.

Recycling and garden ornaments

Nothing went to waste in the original cottage gardens. All sorts of 'junk' was thoughtfully stored in the back of a shed, against the day it might come in handy. And nowadays, a lot of garden ornaments and equipment that were once discarded as rubbish are being used to decorate cottage gardens. Old

ABOVE RIGHT *Rustic hurdles were originally used as temporary sheep folds by shepherds at lambing time, and they make excellent cottage garden fencing today. They look particularly attractive with woody climbers such as honeysuckle (here* Lonicera japonica *'Halliana') growing up them.*

RIGHT *A garden roller, no longer used for lawn maintenance, makes an unusual ornament, especially when surrounded by bluebells.*

terracotta forcing pots, once used for rhubarb or seakale, add an authentic touch to an ornamental vegetable plot. Old clay flower pots, especially the oddly shaped or ornamented ones, or those with drainage holes in the sides, are the latest collectibles for garden decoration. Old well buckets, cast-iron garden rollers, vintage lawnmowers, pieces of agricultural equipment, old chimney pots, and ancient garden furniture all add character to a cottage garden. On a more practical note, old dinner knives from jumble sales are perfect for weeding between cracks in paving.

Cracked flower pots can be held together with a piece of thick wire twisted round the middle, while large broken pots can be laid on their sides and planted up with sempervivums or sedums. The old stone sink, filled with soil, will now be growing alpines in a sunny corner close to the house, and old enamel jugs, sometimes repainted with a pretty floral pattern, will be utilized for watering plants in pots instead of a stark new watering can. Indeed, all sorts of old household containers can be converted to take plants if you make drainage holes in the bottom.

DESIGN AND PLANTING

However natural a cottage garden looks, it still has to be planted. Picturesque scenes of vegetables and flowers growing together, rose-clad arches, seas of haphazardly scattered perennials and herbs, and fruit dripping from aged apple trees do not happen by chance. Setting out to create an orderly muddle takes more thought and preparation than might be suggested by the random effect a successful cottage garden creates.

In this cottage garden, borders of flowers, including Linaria purpurea, Anthemis 'Grallagh Gold', white shasta daisies (Chrysanthemum × superbum) and hemerocallis, screen the vegetable plot from the back of the house, while a straight, grass path leads to a standard apple tree.

Long-term planning

A cottage garden should never be over-designed. The basic plan of the garden should allow for gradual changes to be introduced over the years as the garden grows up round you. Much of the groundwork in the cottage garden is similar to that in a normal garden but the emphasis often falls in a different place. Winter digging, for instance, is replaced in the cottage garden by an initial, thorough soil preparation followed by annual mulching.

Types of soil

Assessing the type of soil you have not only helps you decide how best to treat it, but also indicates which plants are likely to thrive in it. In simple terms, if your soil dries out quickly after rain, and feels gritty when rubbed between the hands, it is a light, sandy soil. Heavy clay soils generally feel sticky when wet and puddles may form which tend to take a long time to drain away. The ideal soil is something between the two.

It is also important to know how acid or alkaline the soil is (this is called the pH factor). Most plants grow reasonably well in a neutral soil, or one that is slightly on the acid or alkaline side of neutral. Soil-testing kits are available but will only give an accurate reading if a truly representative soil sample is taken. The best way to do this is to collect several small quantities of soil from different parts of the garden, taking them from a depth of about 15cm (6in) below the surface rather than from the top layer. Mix these together, and take your sample for testing from that. You can also get a good indication of your soil type by looking at the sort of plants that grow well in the neighbourhood. If rhododendrons and camellias grow well, the soil is almost certainly acid, while gypsophila, pinks (*Dianthus*) and scabious (*Scabiosa*) usually indicate an alkaline soil.

Sandy soils

Light, sandy soils need to have plenty of organic matter, such as animal manure and garden compost, dug in before planting to help the soil retain moisture (see below). As this sort of preparation normally takes place during the winter, there is no point in adding any fertilizer to the soil because, by the time you come to plant in the spring, the fertilizer will have all leached away.

Even when improved, very light soils are notoriously hungry, and organic matter disappears from them very quickly. They need topping up with regular, deep (5cm/2in if possible) organic mulches

Improving the soil

For sandy soil, dig out a trench to one spade's depth, then fork in a layer of well-rotted organic matter at least 5cm (2in) thick and incorporate this to a further spade's depth with a fork (see 1, right). Replace the soil mixed with more organic matter.
For clay soil, spread a 5–8cm (2–3in) layer of coarse sand over the soil and dig it in to one spade's depth (see 2, right).

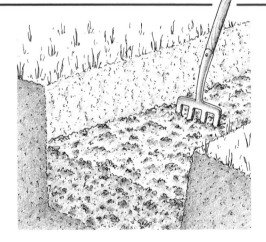

1 *Improving sandy soil*

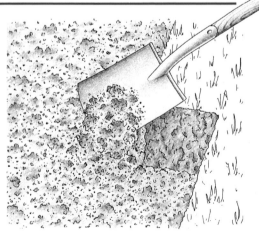

2 *Improving clay soil*

ordinary building sand may contain high levels of lime which can make the soil over-alkaline.

Many clay soils have an impervious layer below the soil surface, the depth of which can vary from 10–50cm (4–20in); this 'subsoil' is generally very infertile and should not be brought up to the surface when digging. It can easily be recognized by its different colour: it is usually lighter than the topsoil, which shows there is less humus in it, and it may have a yellowish or bluish tinge, showing that no oxygen reaches it. Where the topsoil is shallow, do not dig a deep hole when planting trees and shrubs and put organic matter at the bottom, as is normally recommended; instead, fork compost into the topsoil over the whole bed to give new plants a wide, shallow rooting run in good soil.

Using fertilizer

Artificial fertilizers were not used in early cottage gardens as natural fertilizers were freely available (see page 10). Nowadays gardeners are unlikely to have access to enough rich material, so organic matter is supplemented by artificial fertilizers. The most suitable for cottage gardening are described below, and guidance is given on how to use them.

Types of fertilizer

The three main nutrients required by plants are nitrogen (N), phosphorus (P) and potassium (K). These can be supplied either as solid fertilizers, which release their nutrients slowly over a fairly long period of time, or as liquid fertilizers, which release their nutrients quickly over a short period of time. Solid general fertilizers supply these nutrients in roughly equal amounts, making them ideal for general feeding during the growing season, and for use when preparing the ground just before planting in spring or summer. Organic gardeners prefer a general fertilizer of blood, fish and bone. Bonemeal is a good source of phosphorus and useful for establishing trees and shrubs. As it is very slow-acting, it can be used in autumn or winter.

Liquid or soluble feeds should always be used for feeding plants in containers as solid fertilizers may scorch the roots of container-grown plants. A hand-

When planting vegetables, it is a good idea to walk on a length of slatted wood or a plank rather than the prepared soil to prevent it from compacting. A short plank is useful as a straight edge when planting in rows – use a permanent marking pen to give all the popular spacings, such as 15cm (6in) and 30cm (1ft).

every spring (see page 38) and, ideally, in autumn as well. Since the soil will still dry out relatively fast, the plants that will do best are the Mediterranean types of plant, such as artemisias, sedums and shrubby salvia species, as well as many herbs and other drought-tolerant species.

Clay soils

Heavy, clay soils are also much improved by adding plenty of organic matter, which in this case helps to break up the sticky particles and improve the structure of the soil, allowing surplus moisture to drain away. The quickest way of making a lasting improvement is by digging in coarse, gritty sand before planting (see the illustration on the left). Make sure that it is washed horticultural sand, as

Mulching

Once the garden has been planted, the only way of getting any extra organic matter into the soil is by spreading it in a layer over the top and letting the worms pull it down. This technique is called mulching, and has become very popular with gardeners in general since the spread of the organic movement. But cottage gardeners have been using mulches to improve their soil for years. Mulching is beneficial in many ways. Besides slowly increasing the amount of organic matter in the soil, it also retains moisture round plant roots, which is essential in dry summers or when you are unable to water for a period of time. It insulates the roots from extremes of heat and cold, and smothers annual weed seeds, so there is less weeding to do.

All sorts of materials can be used for mulching, including chipped bark, well-rotted animal manures, gravel, spent hops or old mushroom compost. Leafmould is too valuable to be used as a mulch and should be reserved for improving the soil around a collection of choice plants. Black polythene can be used (choose the slitted type so that air can pass through), although it is best reserved for vegetable plots where it does not spoil the look of the garden, unless you plan to cover it with a layer of gravel or chipped bark. But the best mulch for cottage gardening is home-made garden compost, which comes free of charge, looks natural and improves the soil without introducing other people's weeds.

The best time to mulch is in spring, when herbaceous plants have just started to come through the soil, so you can see where they are, but before they cover the ground (see the illustration on the right). The soil must be moist, and free from large and perennial weeds, though small annual weed seedlings will be smothered. Make sure plant labels are not buried when mulching; long labels are safest. If you put in new plants during the growing season, spread mulching material round them after watering them well in. On very hungry, light, sandy soils, it is a good idea to apply a further mulch in autumn, as it is with any large areas of soil that will be left exposed in the winter, when heavy rain could otherwise damage its structure.

Walk-through planting schemes are very difficult to weed if they are not mulched thickly early each spring to smother out annual weed seedlings. Once the foliage covers the ground by early summer, or where the plants are growing close together, weeds are unlikely to establish themselves.

ful of dried blood dissolved in a 9 litre (2 gallon) can of water also makes a good high nitrogen feed useful for brassica plants during the spring and early summer. High potash liquid or soluble tomato feeds should always be used for tomatoes, but are very beneficial (diluted with twice the usual amount of water) for other fruiting or flowering plants in containers, such as fuchsias, and any heavy feeders such as clematis, dahlias and cottage chrysanthemums (*Dendranthema rubellum*).

Rose enthusiasts may prefer to use a specially formulated rose feed which contains magnesium and other trace elements. This can also be used on other shrubs, hedges and fruit trees. However, in a well-run cottage garden, trace elements are provided by the heavy use of organic matter.

Making compost

Lacking most of the sources of organic matter used in early cottage gardens, modern cottage gardeners need to make their own soil conditioner by recycling non-woody garden rubbish (soft prunings, weeds, grass cuttings) and kitchen waste, such as vegetable peelings, to make compost. Persistent perennial weeds, annual weeds in seed and diseased plant material should not be used, neither should woody stems which will take much longer to rot than soft material, thus delaying the time when the compost is ready to spread. Making compost should be a continuous process so that there is always some ready to use whenever you need it: whether to put in a new plant, prepare the soil for a new bed, improve the soil when digging the vegetable plot in winter, or for mulching in spring. To achieve this, you need at least two compost heaps: one rotting down, and another being filled. A third heap, containing only ready-to-use compost, is desirable but not essential.

The traditional method of making compost is to damp the material and stack it up in layers about 15cm (6in) deep, with a few spadefuls of soil or animal manure in between each layer to inoculate it with bacteria. The compost heap needs to be at least 90cm (3ft) high, by the same dimension across and deep, or it will not heat up enough to work properly. It also needs turning at least once, so that the dry material round the outside is moved to the centre where it can rot down. Lawn mowings should be added to the compost heap in layers about 15cm (6in) deep, in between layers of other material. If you have a huge quantity of mowings and little other material, heap the mowings separately and add them to the compost heap a layer at a time as other material becomes available. The first three to four mowings from grass treated with weedkiller should be composted separately for at least six months before being used.

Garden compost is ready to use when it has thoroughly rotted down and its components are no longer recognizable; it does not always look like soil – it can be quite fibrous in texture if coarse materials are used, and somewhat slimy if a lot of soft materials like lawn mowings are used. This will not matter by the time it is on the garden – just dig it in or spread it on the soil, and let nature take its course.

Modern, purpose-made compost bins are the fastest and easiest way of converting garden rubbish into compost. The most efficient type has insulated side panels and lid; this heats up so efficiently that the compost is ready to spread within three months in summer, and even weed seeds are killed. A thrifty alternative would be to cut out the bottom of an old dustbin, metal or plastic, and punch a few holes in the sides to let air in; or you could make your own structure from slatted wood.

Mulching herbaceous plants

Spread garden compost over the exposed soil, taking extra care around the crowns of the plants in order not to smother the young plants (see 1, right). Species such as some hardy cranesbills (*Geranium*) and london pride (*Saxifraga umbrosa*) which have thick stems that persist above ground need to have a handful of compost trickled between their stems to give them more stability. This will also prevent the plants from becoming untidy and succumbing to frost and drought (see 2, right).

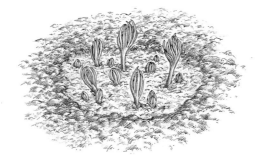

1 *Spread a 2.5–5cm (1–2in) layer of compost carefully over the soil.*

2 *Trickle compost into the centre of plants that 'grow themselves out of the ground'.*

Routine maintenance

Even after planting, a certain amount of routine maintenance is needed. Although weeding and pest control are much less of a chore in the cottage garden than in a normal garden, periodically you will need to spend time thinning out overgrown plants, removing superfluous self-seeders, and cosseting choice plants that require special attention.

Dealing with the weeds

One of the great benefits of having a cottage garden is that there is very little weeding to do. By filling the beds with closely planted perennials, most annual weeds are quickly smothered by the rising tide of foliage. Serious weeding will be needed twice a year, in spring before perennials are big enough to cover the ground, and again in autumn, after the beds have been tidied of dead foliage.

Perennial weeds are more of a problem. Nettles and thistles can be dug out; the real menaces are horsetail, couch grass and ground elder, all of which spread by underground rhizomes. If you try to dig these out, all you do in effect is to propagate them by root cuttings. The intertwining stems of convolvulus cannot be pulled out without also pulling out the plants you wish to keep. These weeds are best controlled by applying a translocated herbicide, such as glyphosate, to their leaves, but do not get any on the surrounding plants.

In theory, if perennial weeds are a real problem, the ground should be left fallow for a year before planting, allowing the weeds to be killed properly with weedkiller or by regular hoeing, or even by mowing. Putting an area badly affected by upright perennial weeds to grass and then mowing regularly removes the leaves above-ground which feed the weeds by photosynthesizing, and the weed roots are thus 'starved out'. However, in practice most people are too impatient to wait a year. Then it is necessary to check regularly all the places you know to be infested, and ruthlessly kill off the shoots of weeds when they appear. Do this with a hoe or spot-treat them with a weedkiller, such as glyphosate.

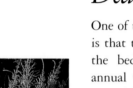

Equisetum arvense
(Horsetail)

Like many weeds found in old cottage gardens, horsetail was put to good use. It contains a high level of silica which gives the stems an abrasive texture. The late sixteenth century herbalist John Gerard describes how the stems, screwed into balls, could be used to clean milkpans and wooden kitchen implements. Pewter was also cleaned in this way – hence the plant's old name of pewterwort. Even now horsetail makes a good emergency scouring pad.

Pests and diseases

Pests and diseases do not usually present too much of a problem in cottage gardens, since the rather basic, unimproved plants that are traditional cottage garden flowers are naturally more disease-resistant than a lot of modern flowers. By growing a wide range of plants, including wild flowers, and leaving the garden unsprayed by chemicals, beneficial insects will automatically colonize the garden. Severe outbreaks of greenfly are rare once a good population of ladybirds, lacewings and hoverflies takes up residence, while ground beetles and centipedes deal with various pests and should never be stamped on.

Chemicals, if used at all, are best saved for difficult perennial weeds and pests that cannot be tackled satisfactorily any other way, such as vine weevils and root aphids. These insects are a threat to your choice primulas, primroses and auriculas, both in pots and in the soil, where they lay their eggs and the larvae eat the roots. The only clue to their presence is when the leaves droop and turn yellow, and by then it is too late. The only way to safeguard against these pests is before the damage occurs, by routinely mixing a little soil insecticide into the holes before planting them up. Any product with 'soil insecticide' on its label is suitable.

Planting and transplanting

The best time for moving plants is in autumn or early spring, though there are exceptions, such as bearded irises which are best moved about six weeks after they finish flowering, in summer. The key to successful transplanting lies in very good soil preparation with plenty of well-rotted organic matter being dug into the new site. If you are transplanting 'out of season', it is absolutely essential to cosset the plant with regular watering while it re-establishes itself, and to give it temporary shelter from wind or sun while its roots settle in.

Trees, shrubs, fruit trees and bushes grown in containers can be planted at any time of year, except when the soil is frozen or muddy. If planted in summer, they will need regular watering until established. Plants sold with bare roots wrapped in sacking must only be planted between leaf-fall and bud-burst, while they are dormant.

Perennial flowers were formerly planted in autumn or spring in order to get established in time for the forthcoming flowering season, but it is now quite common to buy them growing in containers and plant them even when in flower during the summer. Annuals are planted in spring, usually already in bud or flower. It is important to ensure that half-hardy annuals are not planted out before the risk of frost in your area is over. Annuals are pulled out at the end of the season when the last flowers are over. Biennials, such as wallflowers (*Cheiranthus*), sweet williams (*Dianthus barbatus*) and canterbury bells (*Campanula medium*), are planted in late summer to flower the following year. Although many will flower again in subsequent years, the plants become straggly and untidy and should be replaced annually; young plants flower better in any case.

How to plant

The general rule for planting is to dig a hole at least twice the size of the plant's rootball, and to fork plenty of organic matter into the bottom, with a little pre-planting fertilizer (bonemeal in autumn or winter, blood, fish and bone or similar general fertilizer in spring or summer). Remove the container, and gently loosen the biggest roots from the mass so they can spread outwards as soon as they are planted. Stand the plant in position (knock in a stake at this stage if you are planting a tree) and fill in round the roots with a mixture of garden soil and more organic matter. After planting, firm the soil down with your heel and water well. Spread a 2.5–5cm (1–2in) layer of mulching material (see page 39) round the new plant. If you are planting in summer, check periodically for the next few months and water whenever needed to keep the soil moist.

Planting bulbs

The loose skins on all bulbs should be removed before planting; this is particularly important for tulips as it aids rooting. For bulbs planted in autumn, sprinkle bonemeal or proprietary bulb fertilizer and rake in to well-prepared soil (see page 36). If soil pests, such as wireworm, are a problem, mix soil insecticide into the soil. For bulbs planted in spring or summer, use a general fertilizer. Sprinkle bulbs over the soil randomly and plant them wherever they fall for a natural effect. For a formal edging, plant rows of bulbs close together but not quite touching. Using a trowel, plant the bulbs to about twice their own depth, pointed end up, and 'screw' them into the soil to ensure that the basal plate of each bulb makes proper contact with the soil, otherwise they will have difficulty rooting in. Then fill the hole with garden soil; if your soil is heavy, mix with a little grit. On very heavy clay, plant bulbs that are prone to rotting, tulips for example, on 5cm (2in) of grit to prevent water gathering around the base of the bulbs.

An old apple tree, although no longer very productive, helps to disguise a garden shed as well as adding character to the garden. Here, Clematis montana var. rubens has been planted up through the tree to extend the flowering season. This clematis is particularly suited to the task – it makes quite a large climber which needs room to spread, and requires no pruning.

A low-maintenance border

This low-maintenance scheme of self-seeding and fast-spreading plants is perfect if you wish to fill a border in a hurry. The mixture of spring and summer flowers makes it possible for the leaves of the spring flowers to provide a good background of foliage to help set off the summer flowers. The border is shown here in mid-summer.

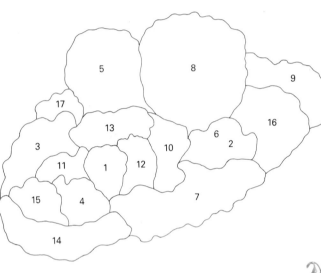

1 *Argyranthemum foeniculaceum*, syn. *Chrysanthemum foeniculaceum*: half-hardy perennial with sprays of feathery, glaucous foliage and masses of neat daisy flowers from early to late summer; 60–90cm (2–3ft) tall.

2 Bachelor's buttons (*Ranunculus acris* 'Flore Pleno'): 90cm (3ft) tall stems of double yellow flowers in early summer; perennial.

3 Borage (*Borago officinalis*): self-seeding hardy annual with masses of blue 'bee' flowers all summer; grows to 60–90cm (2–3ft).

4 Cone flower (*Echinacea pallida*): 90cm (3ft) tall flowers with dark red central boss surrounded by elegant, narrow, pale mauve petals in mid-summer; not a very fast-spreading plant so ensure it is not overwhelmed; herbaceous perennial.

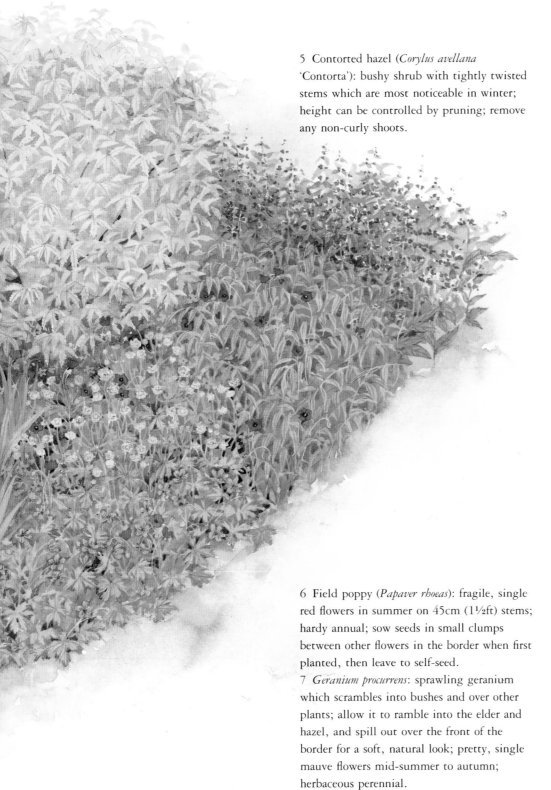

5 Contorted hazel (*Corylus avellana* 'Contorta'): bushy shrub with tightly twisted stems which are most noticeable in winter; height can be controlled by pruning; remove any non-curly shoots.

6 Field poppy (*Papaver rhoeas*): fragile, single red flowers in summer on 45cm (1½ft) stems; hardy annual; sow seeds in small clumps between other flowers in the border when first planted, then leave to self-seed.

7 *Geranium procurrens*: sprawling geranium which scrambles into bushes and over other plants; allow it to ramble into the elder and hazel, and spill out over the front of the border for a soft, natural look; pretty, single mauve flowers mid-summer to autumn; herbaceous perennial.

8 Golden cut-leaved elder (*Sambucus racemosa* 'Plumosa Aurea'): domed shrub with lacy, gold leaves; size easily controlled by pruning.

9 Hedge woundwort (*Stachys sylvatica*): wild flower traditionally grown in cottage gardens; downy leaves and maroon flowers in whorls up the stems mid- to late summer; 60–90cm (2–3ft) tall; good in shade; perennial.

10 *Iris spuria*: 90–120cm (3–4ft) tall, upright, iris leaves with narrow, creamy flowers in early mid-summer; the leaves are a great architectural feature of the bed; herbaceous perennial.

11 *Iris versicolor*: pale blue and purple flowers with yellow flashes in late spring; 60cm (2ft); herbaceous perennial.

12 *Lobelia* 'Queen Victoria': dark red, upright stems of foliage growing to 90cm (3ft) topped by sprays of red lobelia flowers in mid- to late summer; herbaceous perennial.

13 Maltese cross (*Lychnis chalcedonica*): upright stems around 90cm (3ft) tall topped by flattish heads of long-lasting, orange-red, cross-shaped flowers in early to mid-summer; herbaceous perennial.

14 Pennyroyal (*Mentha pulegium*): spreading plant with small leaves like grey-green mint and 30cm (1ft) stems supporting whorls of lavender-blue flowers in early to mid-summer; herbaceous perennial.

15 Rampion (*Campanula rapunculus*): ancient root vegetable and a very pretty garden flower; 75cm (2½ft) spires of blue bells in mid-summer; herbaceous perennial.

16 Solomon's seal (*Polygonatum multiflorum*): 60cm (2ft) arching stems laden with dangling white bells in early summer; good foliage afterwards; herbaceous perennial.

17 Tansy, curled (*Tanacetum vulgare* 'Crispum'): upright stems with stiff 'prince-of-wales' feather foliage topped by yellow button flowers in mid- to late summer; 90cm (3ft); herbaceous perennial.

Establishing the background

The first step when starting a cottage garden is to plan and plant the permanent framework. In any other style of garden this 'backbone' planting would be of evergreen trees and shrubs, but since evergreens do not figure very much in authentic cottage gardens, hedges and deciduous trees, fruit trees and shrubs generally establish the structural framework instead. Although conifers are not considered cottagey, yew (*Taxus*) hedges or topiary are often seen in today's cottage garden.

Boundary hedges

An authentic garden boundary really sets the scene for a cottage garden, and most traditional country cottages would have been surrounded by hedges. Old hedgerows contained a mixture of species (they can still be spotted today), and trees were often allowed to grow up through the hedge, which gave a more interesting outline. Damsons (*Prunus inst11ia*), nut trees such as hazel (*Corylus avellana*), and elderberries (*Sambucus nigra*) were commonly grown in this way, making the hedge a productive asset in its own right. A surrounding hedge or shelter belt (which is basically a hedge that is allowed to grow tall, rather than being clipped) of small trees still looks lovely round a rural cottage garden. It is invaluable for providing shelter in an exposed site, and serves as a green backdrop against which cottage borders show up well, besides attracting birds by providing them with food, perching places and cover. Another useful bonus today is that a dense hedge provides security, especially if thorny species are included. Within the shelter provided by this boundary hedge, groups of ornamental trees or shrubs can be planted for additional wind-filtering effect, if required.

Planting and maintaining hedges

Choose one species for a formal or semi-formal hedge, but a mixture of species for a traditional country hedge. The best time for planting is late autumn or early spring, while the young trees are dormant and leafless. Choose plants under 30cm (1ft) tall, as they will establish better as well as being cheaper to buy. Prepare the ground well by digging a trench one or two spades' depth, and forking plenty of well-rotted organic matter into the bottom. Replace the topsoil, after mixing in more organic matter and a pre-planting fertilizer at the manufacturer's recommended rate, and plant (see below).

After planting, most plants should be cut back to about 15cm (6in) above ground. To train a good,

Creating a traditional hedge

The young plants should be spaced about 30cm (1ft) apart and cut back hard after planting. This will ensure that the hedge is well furnished at its base as well as higher up. If there is room, plant a double row, 30–45cm (1–1½ft) apart, instead of a single one, staggering adjacent plants to give a really solid wall of foliage (see 1, right). In a mixed country hedge, leave an occasional tree unclipped – a holly, elder or hawthorn for instance – to grow up through the top of the hedge as a standard tree (see 2, right).

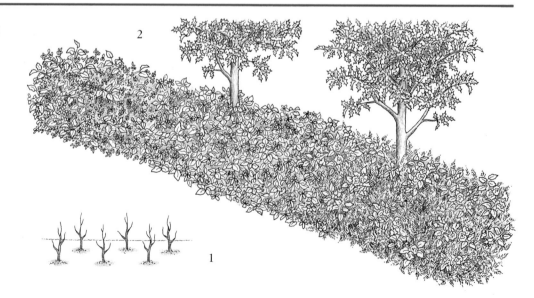

COUNTRY HEDGE
PLANTS
Bird cherry
 (*Prunus padus*)
Blackberry
 (*Rubus fruticosus*)
Damson (*Prunus institia*)
Dog rose (*Rosa canina*)
Eglantine
 (*Rosa rubiginosa*,
 syn. *R. eglanteria*)
Elderberry
 (*Sambucus nigra*)
Guelder rose
 (*Viburnum opulus*)
Hawthorn
 (*Crataegus monogyna*)
Hazel (*Corylus avellana*)
Sloe (*Prunus spinosa*)

dense hedge right from the start, cut the new shoots back frequently to about 5–10cm (2–4in) from their base, every time enough new growth has been made during the growing season. In this way the hedge builds up slowly in 'steps', but fills in from the bottom upwards, with no ugly gaps. If you want a shelter belt, however, leave the leaders intact to give a row of small trees rather than a tightly knit hedge.

Formal hedges such as yew should be cut with shears or an electric hedge-trimmer as often as necessary to keep them looking neat, and the top at the right height. It is a good idea to delay the last cut until after the end of the growing season so that the hedge looks tidy for the winter. For maximum wind resistance, this type of hedge should be cut so that the sides slope very slightly inwards, with the base slightly wider than the top. Semi-formal clipped hedges of, for instance, hawthorn or mixed country species, usually need more frequent cutting than yew, which is relatively slow-growing. To give a more rustic appearance, you could deliberately round the 'shoulders' of the hedge, and leave the top undulating rather than completely level.

A shelter belt and informal flowering hedges such as those grown from rose species, are better pruned than clipped, and even then a minimum of attention is needed. Prune a shelter belt while the trees are dormant and, as a general rule, prune hedges that flower before early summer immediately after flowering. For later flowering hedges (those that flower on shoots produced during the current year), prune in early spring when pruning roses.

This hedge of Lonicera nitida, *trimmed to form an arch over the gate, provides a natural boundary to the garden. In the foreground* Rosa rubiginosa, *the old cottage eglantine, is spiralled round a support framework of three rustic poles to keep its long, thorny stems tidy.*

45

Background planting for large borders

Although cottage gardens are traditionally created for the most part from smaller plants, the large borders that are included in many of today's gardens often need a good background to set them off. Carefully chosen, a background of small trees and ornamental shrubs can also help to extend the border's season of interest. Especially useful are those that flower or provide some other attraction such as decorative foliage outside the peak season for cottage garden flowers (spring and mid-summer). Many cottage gardeners make a point of including trees and shrubs that are not particularly traditional simply because they like them, and yet still manage to achieve an overall cottagey effect. But if you want to ensure a degree of authenticity, choose close relatives of native countryside species, fruiting trees and bushes, shrubby herbs and their relatives, and other species that have traditionally been associated with cottage gardens over the years, as listed below.

Background shrubs

Bay tree (*Laurus nobilis*): slow-growing but in time large shrub or small tree with oval evergreen leaves used in cooking.

Black elder (*Sambucus nigra* 'Purpurea'): large, deciduous shrub with blackish purple leaves; a good background to brightly coloured flowers or foliage.

Bridal wreath (*Spiraea × arguta*): medium to large deciduous shrub which produces masses of small white flowers in spring.

Butterfly bush (*Buddleja*): large, fast-growing, deciduous shrub with pyramidal-shaped mauve, purple or white flowers in summer, which attracts butterflies; needs hard pruning after flowering to retain a tidy shape.

Contorted hazel (*Corylus avellana* 'Contorta'): slow-growing, deciduous shrub with spiralling stems which in time grows large; seen to best effect in winter, when the leaves have fallen.

Crab apple (*Malus* cultivars, for example 'John Downie'): small to medium-sized deciduous tree bearing good crops of blossom in spring and coloured

fruit from late summer through to autumn.

Daphne mezereum: small, deciduous shrub with highly scented purple flowers in early spring.

Eglantine (*Rosa rubiginosa*, syn. *R. eglanteria*) cultivars: windproof, with large, showy pink or white flowers and huge hips.

Flowering currant (*Ribes sanguineum*): small, deciduous aromatic shrub with sprigs of reddish-pink flowers in spring; does not fruit.

Golden elder (*Sambucus racemosa* 'Plumosa Aurea'): large, spectacular, deciduous shrub with big, fringed, golden leaves; sometimes produces spherical, red berries in summer.

Hardy fuchsia (*Fuchsia* 'Riccartonii'): small, upright shrub which dies back to ground level in winter; large dangling red and purple flowers are produced

A softly coloured cottage border of Nicotiana langsdorfii, Sisyrinchium striatum, Achillea *'Moonshine' and* Kniphofia *'Candlelight' is enhanced by a backdrop of roses and honeysuckle.*

throughout the summer and into autumn.

Holly (*Ilex aquifolium*): slow-growing but in time large shrub or tree with evergreen leaves; not all species are prickly.

Jerusalem sage (*Phlomis fruticosa*): small, evergreen shrub with woolly, grey-green leaves, and golden-yellow sage flowers in summer.

Lilac (*Syringa vulgaris* cultivars): large shrubs or medium-sized trees with highly scented pyramid-shaped flowerheads in early summer which are not very weather-resistant.

Mock orange (*Philadelphus*): large, deciduous shrub with scented white flowers in late spring.

Myrtle (*Myrtus communis*): small, evergreen shrub with dark green foliage and fragrant, single white flowers and long stamens in summer.

Ornamental quince (*Chaenomeles*): medium-sized deciduous shrub with green or golden fruit in summer and autumn.

Purple hazel (*Corylus maxima* 'Purpurea'): Deciduous, medium-sized shrub with large purple leaves; nuts are ready to eat in autumn.

Rosa glauca: single pink flowers followed by small hips but mainly grown for its mauvish leaves covered with a pewter 'bloom'.

Rosa moyesii 'Geranium': outstanding displays of flask-shaped, coral-coloured hips.

Rowan or mountain ash (*Sorbus aucuparia* cultivars): medium to large, deciduous tree; usually produces

red berries in late summer and autumn.

Snowberry (*Symphoricarpos*): medium-sized, deciduous shrub with lots of white or pink berries in late summer and autumn, often held into early winter.

Viburnum: family of medium to large shrubs, including both evergreen and deciduous species; many deciduous species have nicely scented pink flowers in early spring and very attractive autumn foliage.

*The golden hop (*Humulus lupulus *'Aureus') clambers up a framework of rustic poles to give height at the back of the border.*

Training climbers up rustic poles

Another successful way to back a large border is to construct a tall framework of rustic poles and use it to grow rambler or climbing roses, clematis or honeysuckle – classic cottage garden climbers. If the framework is at the back of the border, remember to leave a path on either side of the structure, otherwise gaining access for pruning, weeding and structural repairs can become a nightmare. Always avoid growing very tall plants in front of roses or fruit as too much shade will prevent them from performing well.

Dividing up the garden

Boundaries within gardens do not have to be very solid; anything that screens or even just filters the next part of the garden from view is sufficient. A row of half-standard apple trees, whose branches barely touch, is all that is needed to interrupt your line of sight.

Faced with a vast empty plot, it can be very daunting to set about carving up the garden into the series of smaller areas that most cottage gardens ultimately become. However, once the first divisions have been made, the rest follows on much more easily. Most cottage gardens do not follow a strict plan, but rather grow up gradually around their owner, continually being altered and added to, so it may take many years to arrive at their final form. A good way to find initial inspiration is by visiting as many established cottage gardens as you can, to see how they are set out. Then make a rough sketch plan of your own garden, and play around with a few alternative ways of how it might be divided up.

Garden features

The garden's natural vagaries of shape often provide a good starting place, which is why odd-shaped gardens can be easier to deal with than rectangular ones. Get some idea of the features you want to include from the outset. If you want an area in which to grow fruit and vegetables, this is traditionally separated off towards the end of the garden. You might want a paved seating area, and a sunny spot close to the house is most suitable for this. How about a herb garden, a long border, or a rose walk? At this stage it is best to plan for a mixture of distinct areas linked by walks, and then to position 'structural' plants to echo the shape, leaving the detail of what goes inside the different areas to be filled in later.

All sorts of plants and other garden elements make good interior dividers. Hedges are an obvious choice, from formal clipped ones such as box or yew, informal flowering ones such as species roses or flowering currant, or miniature hedges of lavender or rosemary (*Rosmarinus officinalis*). A dense specimen tree or shrub or a solid-looking group of plants can help to separate one part of the garden from another by creating a visual break – try, for instance, a topiary tree, a group of trimmed box (*Buxus semper-virens*), a clump of *Euphorbia characias wulfenii* or a striking specimen tree like a mulberry (*Morus*), edible quince (*Cydonia oblongata*) or medlar (*Mespilus*). Architectural features, like a climber-clad arch or a row of rustic hurdles, can also be used to separate the various components that make up the garden.

Garden divisions do not have to be high. A change of surface underfoot, from grass to gravel, or from gravel to brick, creates just as much of a change of character as a vertical feature. It is a good idea in any case to use garden divisions of varying heights – too many tall ones make a garden seem small and dark. When you do use tall dividers, especially in a small garden, keep the effect light by cutting peepholes through a hedge, or by using trees with light canopies of foliage such as birch (*Betula*) or open-work structures like a rustic fence.

Traditional paths

In the past, cottagers created temporary paths wherever they were needed, simply by tipping the clinker and ashes from their fires on to muddy patches anywhere they regularly walked, until a path evolved. The most common routes were along the front of the house, out to the woodshed, the vegetable garden, the wash-house or privy, and along the washing line. Since new ashes were being produced all the time – the fire was kept burning all year round for cooking and to supply hot water – path materials were always available.

The same principle is applied by many of today's cottage gardeners, using gravel, stone slabs, paving stones or old bricks. Gravel can simply be tipped straight on to the soil wherever you want a path, and retained by an edging of bricks or wooden shuttering. However, for greater stability, gravel paths can also have a base of hardcore. In the cottage garden most gravel paths start out as grass paths, then are gravelled over when they become muddy from frequent use. Bricks require a little more effort, as they need to be sunk into the ground for most of their depth to keep them steady. Bricks that become loose should be lifted and gravel or small stones tamped in the ground. Replace the bricks and tamp soil firmly round them, using the head of a sledgehammer. Paving slabs need nothing more than just setting into the ground as their size and weight make them stable. Such temporary paths are perfectly adequate for wheelbarrows and are also very easy to take up and replace. Cottage garden paths should never look as if they have been produced by a machine, and any levelling should be done by eye, otherwise the overall cottagey effect will be spoiled.

Permanent paths

Although paths in cottage gardens are not meant to be permanent – they certainly are not traditional and will impede any changes you may wish to make to the garden in the future – seating areas and paths that receive regular, heavy use are best made with proper foundations.

After excavating to the required depth – allow for the thickness of the paving slab or brick surface, 2.5cm (1in) of sand and at least 5cm (2in) of coarser material, such as coarse gravel or small broken stones – flatten the earth base of the path and pack it down hard. A layer of coarse material should then be spread over the bottom and tamped down firmly, followed by a layer of builder's sand, making sure that all is still level. Bricks or paving slabs can be laid directly on to the sand or on to three (when laying bricks) or five (when laying slabs) blobs of mortar. Place spacers between adjacent slabs as when tiling a wall to ensure even gaps between them. These are filled with mortar afterwards.

This simple path of stepping stones, sunk into the soil, is flanked by a dwarf box hedge (Buxus sempervirens 'Suffruticosa'), red poppies (Papaver) and white stonecrop (Sedum acre). The stones can easily be lifted should you wish to alter the layout of the garden.

Regular and irregular plots

A changing sequence of small cameo gardens, each with a distinct theme of its own, gives interest to a regularly shaped plot. The chamomile lawn in the foreground of the picture, bordered by box hedging, leads to a herb garden.

A good cottage garden should leave you wondering what you cannot see, as well as enjoying what you can. It needs planning in such a way that only part of the garden is visible from the house, and even when you start walking around, there should be several nooks and crannies to explore, and surprises to discover round bends in the path. Even when you know the garden well, it should still provide fresh discoveries, with an ever-changing succession of new flowers coming into bloom.

Old cottages usually have interesting, irregularly shaped gardens, thanks to centuries of buying and selling land with neighbours, building on to the cottage itself, and alterations to the road outside. The end result is often a dog-leg shape which naturally lends itself to being developed as a series of separate areas, linked by paths which meander round a series of obstacles that change with time.

Newer cottages, however, were often built on dull, oblong plots which present a real challenge to the imagination. Lacking natural idiosyncracies, the only answer is to create some of your own. There are several useful techniques that help, such as dividing the garden up into compartments using internal divisions (see page 20). By breaking up the geometric outline, you automatically create a feel of the sort of irregularity that happens naturally in an old cottage garden.

The main problem when faced with a bare, oblong plot is deciding where to start. One method you could use is to look out of the different windows of the house and imagine what you would like to see through them. While it is not really practical to arrange a totally different view from each one, it is a good ideal at which to aim. A popular formula is to have an open area immediately behind the house, usually grassed with borders around it and perhaps a specimen tree forming a focal point, with a seating area underneath it. This is often partially enclosed by the surrounding borders, with paths leading off it to different parts of the garden. These may lead to dead-ends furnished with a seat and a good view, or perhaps to a 'theme' garden of some sort (see page 60). Some paths might lead through open space, perhaps a patch of orchard underplanted with spring bulbs, or to the vegetable plot. They may double back on themselves, taking you on 'stepping stones' through a carpet of low ground cover broken up by taller plants, perhaps to a secret garden bordered by hedges. A key ingredient shared by most successful cottage gardens is roughly to alternate enclosed space with open space, to keep your view constantly changing as you walk round.

How to create interest

This plan shows how a cottage garden might look when first set up; it requires little maintenance and is suitable for a family as there is plenty of lawn and some uncultivated areas where children can play. There is also a quiet corner filled with herbs and scented plants where the adults can sit in peace. As the family grows up there is scope for the garden to evolve to suit the changing needs of its owners – something all good cottage gardens should do (see page 81 for an idea of how this garden may appear several years on).

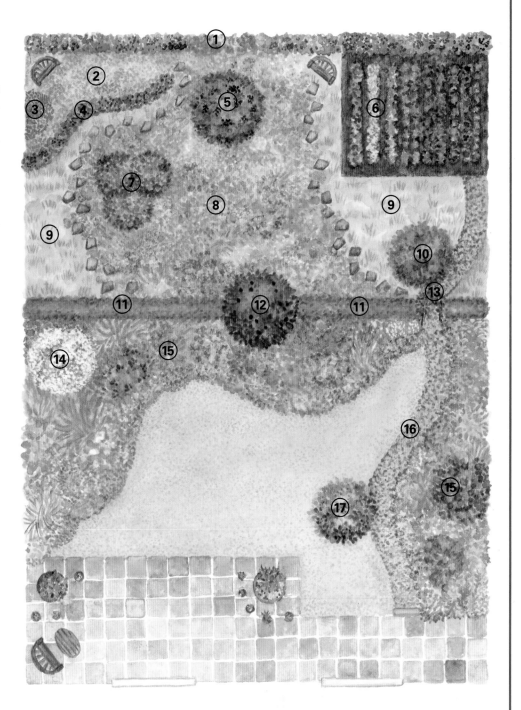

1 *Fruiting hedge*
2 *Herb lawn*
3 *Herb bed*
4 *Yew hedge*
5 *Elder*
6 *Vegetable garden*
7 *Apple trees*
8 *Carpet of spreading and self-seeding plants*
9 *Rough grass and spring bulbs*
10 *Quince*
11 *Box hedge*
12 *Medlar*
13 *Rose arch*
14 *Flowering cherry*
15 *Cottage border*
16 *Gravel path*
17 *Mulberry*

Plants as features

Something as unexpected as this formal topiary shape, tucked in between an informal mixture of plants and under an old fruit tree, helps to keep a cottage garden full of surprises. Box is the most suitable topiary plant to grow in a shady spot such as this.

As well as 'hard' rustic features (see page 22), a cottage garden may contain several different plant features, where, for example, trees and shrubs have been trained into distinctive shapes to make a focal point in a particular area. These types of plant are not only fun to own and train, but also add a great deal to the character of the garden.

Feature trees

A tree, provided it is an interesting shape, is a good way of making a focal point in the middle of a lawn. Gnarled old apple trees, or other similar fruit trees, with leaning trunks or branches held up by wooden props are particular favourites in cottage gardens.

They may be used to support a swing or hammock, or a permanent seat might be built around the base of the trunk. To provide summer flowers and compensate for the lack of fruit, a clematis can be planted close by and encouraged to ramble up through the tree's branches. Other fruit trees that have an interesting outline include mulberry which has craggy bark and makes a good, spreading shape, the eating sort of quince, like 'Vranja' which has a more interesting form than the much smaller and bushier ornamental quince, and medlar, a good-looking tree whose leaves colour up in autumn. Even an elder, with a good, spreading 'head', looks the part.

Topiary

Formally clipped trees such as holly would have featured in traditional cottage gardens growing up through hedges and trimmed into a variety of shapes. Topiary, however, is an idea the more recent romantic school of cottage gardeners borrowed from the formal, grand gardens of the past, but it is well worth including in today's cottage garden. A topiary tree makes an imposing specimen in the middle of a small gravelled or grassed front garden; always keep the size in proportion to that of the house, or the effect will look uncomfortable. In a secret garden at the back of the house, it is fun to discover on a lawn something with a touch of humour, like a pair of pecking peacocks. Less ornate topiary specimens, like a row of tightly clipped, flame-shaped trees, are a good way of filtering out part of the view from a path, so you have to continue to the end to see round them. (See also page 82 for creating topiary.)

Climbers for walls

Climbing roses, wisteria and large-flowered clematis such as *Clematis* 'Jackmanii' are all popular and traditional choices for climbers, although in some ways it seems a pity to waste the protection a wall offers by growing anything other than choice or slightly tender shrubs that would not thrive without shelter. If you avoid brash, modern-looking plants,

MAKING A JASMINE PORCH

Screw vine eyes into the front of the porch and attach trellis or rigid netting to them. If the jasmines are leggy, cut them back after planting to encourage branching. Tie the strong shoots up to the trellis or netting, spreading them out evenly. As new shoots grow out, away from the wall, clip them back to within 5–8cm (2–3in) of their base. Growth will build up in stages until the front of the porch is covered. Clip round the sides of the jasmines to keep them neat, and clip the front after flowering each spring. If the jasmines are clipped in late summer, they may not flower the next spring.

in favour of those with flowers that have an old-fashioned look, you will still end up with an acceptably cottagey feel. Go for the self-clinging climbers such as *Hydrangea petiolaris*, or the rare *Schizophragma hydrangeoides* provided the wall is sound. Ceanothus need training to keep them as flat bushes against a wall, as do pyracantha. The pine-apple broom (*Cytisus battandieri*) will make the most of a prime planting site in a sunny spot.

Plant porches

A very old tradition, dating from before the days cottages had brick-built porches and the front door led straight into the living room, was to create a living porch from shrubs. Winter jasmine (*Jasminum nudiflorum*) was most commonly used this way, trained and clipped into shape to make a solid pillar, probably no deeper than 45cm (1½ft), either side of the door, and which met over the top. Trellis, as we know it, would not have been available so the jasmine was most likely supported by tying its main branches to nails knocked into the cottage walls. I know of one old cottage that still has its jasmine porch, always kept immaculately clipped. It is possible to create the feel of such an old plant porch by using your existing brick or stone porch and growing two winter jasmines, one on either side, and training them up and around the front of the porch. That will still leave the sides of the porch free for climbing roses.

An archway makes a perfect frame for the view beyond. Make the most of it by adding a climber such as Rosa 'Albertine', and give the view a focal point with a strategically placed container. Here, an old lead cistern has been planted with the silver-leaved Convolvulus cneorum. The pink-flowered wall shrub is the slightly tender Abelia × grandiflora.

53

Traditional plant associations

The shocking pink rambler rose 'Dorothy Perkins' has been trained out along wires and mingled with Clematis 'Lasurstern'. In the foreground, a row of 'The Fairy', a small shrub rose, makes a contrasting edging. This group forms the boundary to a front garden, but it would also make an excellent backdrop to a low border.

Certain types of plant are traditionally associated with cottage gardens, but to some extent it is also the way they are put together that helps create the familiar cottage garden style. Below are some tried and tested plant groupings for different situations that have worked well over the years, either in my own garden or in gardens that I know well.

Wall plants

Self-seeded wallflowers (*Cheiranthus*), snapdragons (*Antirrhinum*), stonecrop (*Sedum acre*), pennywort (*Umbilicus rupestris*), yellow corydalis and ivy-leaved toadflax (*Cymbalaria muralis*) look very natural growing out of an old garden wall in a sunny situation. Simply sprinkle seed from nearby plants on to the crumbling old brick and stone, where particles of soil will have lodged in flaking surfaces. If none of the right plants is growing nearby, use packet seed,

but choose species rather than cultivars. Unlike seed taken from nearby plants, which are already adapted to the growing conditions in your area, packet seed need optimum growing conditions.

Modern walls with cemented joints do not provide the necessary nooks and crannies, but you can 'build' plants into a new dry stone wall if you do this as you pile up the stones. You need to pack soil round the plant roots as you build the wall up; trying to press them into pockets afterwards does not work as the roots are invariably left hanging in a pocket of air the other side. Alternatively, make a hollow-topped wall, using a double course of bricks, and fill the centre with soil so that you can plant into it.

Plants for shade

Most traditional cottage garden plants are sun lovers, but what can you grow in the shady corners? *Alchemilla mollis*, *Iris foetidissima*, and *Euphorbia robbiae* look good together; for a bigger group, you could add hellebores, variegated honesty (*Lunaria annua* 'Variegata'), mourning widow geranium (*Geranium phaeum*) and a carpet of *Viola labradorica*. A collection of hardy ferns with varying leaf shapes looks good in a shady position. A carpet of mind-your-own-business (*Soleirolia soleirolii*, syn. *Helxine soleirolii*) – but watch this plant carefully as it is invasive – and/or sweet woodruff (*Asperula odorata*), looks effective planted under a hydrangea.

Few roses will thrive on a wall that gets no sun or on a shady arch, so the few that do are doubly valuable. These include *Rosa* 'Souvenir du Docteur Jamain' (wine red), 'Bleu Magenta' (rich mauve) and 'Russell's Cottage Rambler' (reddish mauve). Quite a few clematis tolerate some shade though they perhaps flower less freely than they might if given more light; 'Nelly Moser' (pink striped), 'Barbara Jackman' (pale mauve), 'Comtesse de Bouchaud' (pink), and 'Hagley Hybrid' (terracotta-pink) all tolerate a shady north-facing wall in my garden. You could add *Lilium* 'Mabel Violet', which has strongly scented pale mauve flowers – a real stunner.

Climbing plants

The most successful combinations are based on an old-fashioned mixture of colours – traditionally pink and mauve. If you are planting several different clematis together in the same spot, choose cultivars that all need the same sort of pruning – either none at all, such as large flowered hybrids that flower twice a year, for example *Clematis* 'Nelly Moser' and the majority of species clematis, or those which are all cut right down to almost ground level in very early spring, such as *C.* 'Jackmanii'. Otherwise, separating out the various stems will be an impossible task. You could also try sweet peas (*Lathyrus odoratus*) and clematis, or a mixture of annual climbers, such as sweet peas, *Rhodochiton atrosanguineus* and morning glory (*Ipomoea purpurea*); *Asarina barclayana* and canary creeper (*Tropaeolum peregrinum*) are also good for fast cover.

Spring interest

While high summer is the peak season for cottage garden flowers, spring is the second most important in terms of display. Flowering cherries underplanted with daffodils, and hazel nut trees surrounded by a carpet of short rough grass in which are growing naturalized dog's tooth violets (*Erythronium dens-canis*), snake's head fritillary (*Fritillaria meleagris*) and wood anemone (*Anemone nemorosa*), with miniature narcissus species, make a wonderful show in spring. And try frills of squills (*Scilla campanulata*) round the base of any individual large trees. In flower borders, wallflowers and parrot tulips go together especially well, as do *Euphorbia characias wulfenii* and large-flowered daffodils. Try also *Brunnera macrophylla* with bluebells (*Hyacinthoides non-scripta*); this combination makes a good weed-suppressing ground cover for light shade.

A hot, dry bank

Many gardens have their problem areas, and a hot, dry bank, where the soil dries quickly after rain and is parched all summer, with the plants blasted by hot sun, can be a particularly difficult situation. But you could try smothering it with clumps of different daffodils in spring, later allowing it to become a riot of self-sown borage (*Borago officinalis*), climbing nasturtiums (*Tropaeolum*) and field poppies (*Papaver rhoeas*) fighting for space with *Lychnis chalcedonica*, tansy (*Tanacetum vulgare*), and both yellow and white daisy-flowered anthemis. Building up such a bank at the end of the garden is, incidentally, a great way to get rid of woody garden rubbish and leafy waste in autumn; just throw a few barrowfuls of soil over it the following spring and sow or plant this sort of mixture to be sure of smothering weeds and having a colourful, low-maintenance area. Bulbs should not be planted, though, until the bank is completed. Tough woody stems can take years to break down, but the bank settles slowly with more material being added, when available, every autumn or winter.

LEFT *Spring bulbs make more of a splash grouped together than dotted around the garden. Dog's tooth violet (*Erythronium dens-canis*), lesser celandine (*Ranunculus ficaria*) and the smallest and earliest of the trumpet daffodils,* Narcissus asturiensis, *make a striking plant association for light shade in moist soil.*

Symphytum officinale (Common comfrey)

Knitbone, the old country name for common comfrey, is grown nowadays for its drooping, purplish, bell-shaped flowers rather than for the medicinal properties it was said to possess, such as healing broken bones and reducing swelling in bruised or sprained limbs. Cherubim and seraphim is a charming country name for the close relative Symphytum grandiflorum, *another old cottage plant which has burnt orange-tipped cream flowers in early spring.*

55

Making a cottage border

Most people know what a cottage border looks like, but when it comes to creating one from scratch, it can be extremely difficult to know where to begin. You can, of course, copy successful borders from other gardens, or, better still, find a good, basic idea and adapt it to your taste by substituting some of your own choices of plants; this way you will end up with a more personal garden. However, once you have gained a little experience in putting plants together, you will feel confident enough to create schemes that are completely your own.

Grouping plants

When stocking a new border, I find that it is a good idea to start by assembling a small group of plants that go together well, then make other good groupings, and finally find a way of linking them together. A simple and effective way to achieve this is to have the same plant cropping up again and again throughout a border, to pull the different groups together. The 'link' plant needs to be something fairly in-

nocuous that you can stand seeing repeatedly, and which remains effective throughout most of the border's season of interest, such as *Astrantia major*, *Alchemilla mollis*, or informal clumps of one of the traditional cottagey annuals in either mixed or single colours – the choice depends very much on the style and degree of formality of your border. I have used borage, for example, as a link plant in a tall, rather wild-looking border, but in a more restrained scheme candytuft (*Iberis coronaria*), godetia or clarkia would be a less conspicuous link. Alternatively, you could use a group of plants like cranesbills (*Geranium*), or a particular colour such as soft yellow or mauve (white is much too harsh). Red, orange and bright yellow plants, which scream for attention, should be avoided as link plants.

When adding a new plant to an existing border, try standing it, still in its pot, in several different positions in the border for a day or so at a time, to judge the effect it has on the established plants and to decide where it will look best. Alternatively, pick some of the flowers and stand them in jam jars of water in each of the possible positions, while you make up your mind.

Using foliage

In many gardens, the most natural link is formed by the foliage of plants that are either still to flower or whose flowers are over. When a border contains a lot of plants flowering over a long season, it is inevitable that some are in flower when others are not, and by planning a carefully interlocked display of late-spring, mid-summer and late-summer flowers, you can rely on the foliage of those that are not in flower to pull together those that are. But keep things fairly flexible, so the border looks natural rather than regimented, and so that you will still be able to tuck in the odd find from a plant-hunting trip at a later stage, without ruining the effect.

Reliable cottage garden plants

The key to creating a good cottage border is to use a mixture of plant shapes and foliage textures, as well

*Chives (*Allium schoenoprasum*) and golden marjoram (*Origanum vulgare 'Aureum'*) give a well-defined edge to a border planting of roses, lilies, campanula and nepeta.*

as flower colours. A good, basic recipe for a summer border might go roughly as follows. Start with tall upright spikes like delphiniums, lupins, *Campanula pyramidalis* and verbascum, which contrast well with the rounded shapes of oriental poppies (*Papaver orientale*) and peonies. Then add linear shapes like bearded iris and day lily (*Hemerocallis*), flat-topped *Achillea filipendulina* 'Gold Plate', and light, airy 'fillers' like *Verbena bonariensis*, *Salvia microphylla* (syn. *S. grahamii*), gypsophila, and *Thalictrum delavayi* (syn. *T. dipterocarpum*) 'Hewitt's Double'. Sprinkle around some large trumpet flowers such as lilies, lots of short spikes such as *Salvia superba* or *Polygonum affine*, and daisy shapes such as dahlias, cottage chrysanthemums and also shasta daisies (*Chrysanthemum × superbum*).

Finish off the front of your border with low, carpeting flowers such as hardy cranesbills (*Geranium* species), lavenders and *Santolina virens*. It is by no means essential to stick to the old maxim about planting 'tallest at the back, shortest at the front'; indeed, this makes for a very artificial, flat-fronted border. It is much more interesting to have taller plants standing out from among surrounding shorter ones. This more random approach also looks much less contrived, and therefore more cottagey. To look authentic, bear in mind that cottage borders need to be well filled with plants; you should not be able to see any bare soil between them by mid-summer. This also helps smother out weeds. Forget textbook spacings and really pack the plants in for a traditionally abundant cottagey look.

Adding roses

No cottage garden could be considered complete without roses. Modern roses, such as Hybrid Teas and Floribundas, flower continuously from early summer into the autumn, and though some people do plant them in cottage gardens, enthusiasts usually prefer old-fashioned roses which are more in keeping with the character of a traditional cottage garden (see also pages 27 and 93, and the planting plan of an old-fashioned rose garden on pages 94–5).

Old-fashioned roses require a different style of planting from Hybrid Teas. This is because they flower for only about four to six weeks in early to mid-summer, and it makes sense to plant them in a border with a spread of flowers that makes a good display for much of the time when the roses are not out. There are all sorts of possible schemes for planting roses, but I particularly like roses growing in a knee-high carpet of plants like hardy cranesbills, shrubby salvias or low, spreading campanulas, with occasional taller perennials such as mallows (*Malva*) at the back of the border and odd clumps of tall plants such as lilies, *Verbascum bombyciferum*, *Verbena bonariensis* and thalictrum between the roses.

Especially in a hot summer, a lot of cottage garden flowers 'go over' early, leaving a long dull gap in the colour scheme from mid-season onwards. By using more late-flowering plants, you can keep the colour coming on well after the roses are over (see the planting plan on pages 94–5).

The flowering meadow style of planting looks most effective in 'wild' areas of the garden. To work well, you need a limited number of plant types, of different shapes and colours, repeated throughout the chosen area. The plants here include monkshood (Aconitum), lupins, roses and sweet rocket (Hesperis matronalis).

A cottage border

This colour scheme, with its pinks, mauves and purples, is a traditional cottage garden favourite planned for mid- to late summer/early autumn interest. Such a border would go well in a small garden with a collection of old-fashioned roses, taking over the interest as the roses finish flowering. It could also be used as the basis of a bigger border with an extended flowering season by alternating the plants shown here with early summer flowering kinds, such as *Silene dioica* 'Rubra Plena' and *Heuchera sanguinea*. The foliage from these would then act as a foil for the later flowers. The border is shown here in late summer.

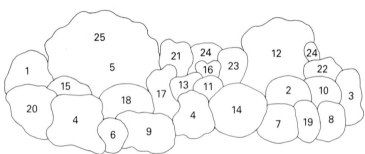

1 *Anemone japonica* (syn. *A. × hybrida*) 'Hadspen Abundance': 60–90cm (2–3ft) high herbaceous perennial with single pink flowers in late summer and early autumn.

2 *Artemisia* 'Powis Castle': 60cm (2ft) non-flowering silver filigree foliage plant; herbaceous perennial.

3 *Astrantia major* 'Margery Fish': shaggy green and white petalled flowers throughout the summer and autumn; grows to 90cm (3ft); herbaceous perennial.

4 *Astrantia major rubra*: deep pink flowers through summer and autumn; grows to 45cm (1½ft); herbaceous perennial.

5 *Clematis viticella* 'Purpurea Plena Elegans':

an old clematis; tight, double, parma violet flowers like small rosettes in late summer.

6 *Diascia* 'Ruby Field': 30cm (1ft) high spreading plant; short spikes of coppery pink flowers all summer; herbaceous perennial.

7 *Geranium* 'Ann Folkard': 30cm (1ft) high scrambling stems with yellow-green foliage and single magenta flowers mid-summer to autumn; herbaceous perennial.

8 *Geranium endressii* 'Wargrave Pink': 30cm (1ft) mounds of foliage; silvery pink flowers mid- to late summer; herbaceous perennial.

9 *Geranium himalayense* 'Plenum': 30cm (1ft) high, leafy mats with an abundance of double purplish flowers from early to late

summer; herbaceous perennial.

10 *Gypsophila pacifica*: glaucous, angular stems, to 120cm (4ft); narrow foliage and masses of tiny, semi-double pink to mauve flowers all summer; herbaceous perennial.

11 Kale 'Russian Red': striking mauve stems with mauve-tinted, frilly leaves; edible shoots in early spring; annual; 90–120cm (3–4ft).

12 *Lavatera* 'Barnsley': shrubby tree mallow with large, pale pink flowers from mid-summer to autumn; deciduous shrub reaching a height of 1.5–2.5m (5–8ft).

13 *Lythrum virgatum* 'The Rocket': spires of mauve and deep pink flowers mid- to late summer; 90cm (3ft); herbaceous perennial.

14 *Nepeta* 'Six Hills Giant': 60cm (2ft) high sprawling catmint with lavender-blue flowers mid- to late summer; herbaceous perennial.

15 *Penstemon* 'Sour Grapes': 75cm (2½ft) spikes topped by groups of purple, grape and amethyst trumpet flowers mid-summer to autumn; herbaceous perennial.

16 *Phlox paniculata* 'Amethyst': amethyst flowers mid- to late summer; herbaceous perennial growing to 90cm (3ft).

17 *Phlox paniculata* 'Sandringham': pink flowers with darker pink centres mid- to late summer; herbaceous perennial; 90cm (3ft).

18 *Salvia × superba*: 90cm (3ft) tall spikes of violet-purple flowers from mid- to late summer; herbaceous perennial.

19 *Salvia superba* 'East Friesland': a dwarf version of the above; 45cm (1½ft) high.

20 *Sedum spectabile* 'Autumn Joy' ('Herbstfreude'): thick, succulent, glaucous foliage and flat green buds that persist for several months before the bright pink flowers open in late summer and autumn; herbaceous perennial; 60cm (2ft) high.

21 *Sidalcea* 'William Smith': 1.2–1.5m (4–5ft) herbaceous perennial flowering in mid-summer; mallow-like flowers in a most attractive and unusual dusky pink.

22 *Strobilanthes atropurpureus*: unusual plant with lots of small, curved, lavender-blue to mauve, trumpet-shaped flowers in mid- to late summer; herbaceous perennial; 90cm (3ft) high.

23 *Thalictrum delavayi* (syn. *T. dipterocarpum*) 'Hewitt's Double': masses of tiny double, mauve-lavender flowers in mid- to late summer around wiry, upright 90cm (3ft) stems; herbaceous perennial.

24 *Verbena bonariensis*: tall (1.5m/5ft) upright stems topped by small blobs of purple flowers in summer and autumn; grows as a biennial in my garden but seeds itself sparingly.

25 *Viburnum rhytidophyllum*: domed evergreen shrub; large oval, leathery, wrinkled leaves.

Theme areas

Whereas other styles of garden rely on large lawns to set off flower beds, cottage gardens, which do not have so much lawn, rely more on contrasts between flowers and hard features such as paths, seats and ornaments to provide the interest. One of the characteristic features of today's cottage garden planting is the creation of themes or of little 'cameos' – groups of plants with a distinct feature, architectural or otherwise – as their focal point. These can blend in naturally with the main garden, or be slightly set apart, almost as secret gardens, by surrounding hedges or banks of shrubs.

All sorts of themes are possible: a water garden, a paved area with plants in containers, a garden on a single colour scheme, or one based round a collection of a particular type of plant, such as a rose garden – there are plenty of opportunities. Such themes make any garden, however small, all the more interesting.

Water as a theme

Ponds in cottage gardens need to look natural, so they are best backed with a tall jungle of wild and wild-looking flowers. Mine has a border of hemp agrimony (*Eupatorium cannabinum*), water figwort (*Scrophularia aquatica*), fullers teasel (*Dipsacus fullonum sylvestris*), *Lythrum virgatum* 'The Rocket' and *Inula magnifica*, planted right up close to the pond so the giant *Inula* leaves are just dipping into the water. These plants are best planted in soil to which organic matter, but no fertilizer, has been added, as fertilizer will turn the water green. Sunk into place on the planting shelves in the shallow water round the edge of the pond, I have dwarf reedmace (*Typha minima*), *Iris laevigata* cultivars and flowering rush (*Butomus umbellatus*) growing in special water plant containers. These should be filled with garden soil that is free

Only natural-looking ponds look right in cottage gardens. Here, turf has been run right down to the water's edge at the front, while wild waterside flowers such as marsh marigold (Caltha palustris), lythrum and hemp agrimony (Eupatorium cannabinum) add height at the back. In the water are a waterlily (Nymphaea), the yellow-fringed waterlily (Nymphoides peltata) which has small leaves and fringed flowers in summer and Ranunculus lingua, a late spring-flowering marginal plant for shallow water with flowers resembling those of a buttercup.

from fertilizer. A couple of small water lilies (*Nymphaea* hybrids), not wild ones which grow far too big, grow in the same kind of pot, sunk in the middle of the pond as they require deeper water, and floating fairy moss (*Azolla*) mingles with canadian pondweed (*Elodea canadensis*) coming up to the surface. Canadian pondweed is the most efficient oxygenator as it is evergreen and works all year round. In less than a year, this collection of plants turned a newly dug pond into what looked like a natural feature.

If you do not have a natural pond, you can create one using either a pre-formed fibreglass liner or butyl or other heavy-duty liner. With pre-formed fibreglass liners, the excavated hole should first be lined with sand to protect the liner from any sharp stones. Soil is then filled in round the liner and tamped down firmly. If you are using a butyl or similar heavy-duty liner (not plastic), use a hosepipe to experiment with various shapes and then as a guide for cutting the outline of the shape. Before putting the liner in place, line the hole with a thick layer of old carpet or newspaper for protection. Both types of pond look better if their edges are hidden, and this is best achieved by a surround of pebbles and low-spreading waterside plants such as water forget-me-nots (*Myosotis scorpioides*) and mimulus.

Colour themes

The white garden at Sissinghurst in Kent is a good place to gather ideas on how to put a limited colour scheme together. When you examine the garden closely, you discover that white has been joined by silver, grey and green foliage, variegated leaves, and flowers in cream, green and palest lilac, as well as white, to give depth to the picture. But the real secret of success is the tremendous range of different shapes, sizes and textures of both foliage and flowers used to contrast with each other.

In a small garden, limited colour schemes are best kept to a small area, or else incorporated within a larger border. Gertrude Jekyll, for instance, once planned a border whose colours graduated from one

end to the other through a sequence of different-coloured plant associations. The darkest colours were at either end, with the brightest, eye-catching reds, oranges and yellows in the middle.

Experimenting with different colour schemes can be great fun, particularly if you do not mind making mistakes and moving plants about until you arrive at the best possible combination. The key is to start with a few favourite plants, or ones you particularly want to grow, and find suitable partners for them. Once you have a basic starting point, you can keep adding to it to make a whole border, or you can link several different 'colour cameos' together to use within a multi-coloured border. Some of my favourite colour associations include:

Red: *Salvia fulgens* and *S. microphylla* (syn. *S. grahamii*) with deep red pompon dahlias.

Yellow: *Euphorbia characias wulfenii*, *Paeonia mlokosewitschii* and daffodils (*Narcissus*).

Green: *Nicotiana langsdorfii*, *Galtonia viridiflora* and gardener's garters (*Phalaris arundinacea* var. *picta*), or, in shade, hart's tongue fern (*Asplenium scolopendrium*, syn. *Phyllitis scolopendrium*), solomon's seal (*Polygonatum*) and *Alchemilla mollis*.

A colour scheme based on mauves and pinks is very restful. Such a scheme has been created using Liatris spicata, Allium sphaerocephalon, Eryngium × tripartitum and Phlox paniculata 'Franz Schubert'. Self-sown opium poppies (Papaver somniferum) have been left to come up where they will.

A yellow colour theme

A yellow border is restful to look at, yet the wide range of highly distinctive architectural shapes available among yellow flowering plants gives scope for creating imaginative planting schemes which do not need a lot of space. This plan, shown in mid-summer, can be a cameo inside a bigger border, or a small bed in its own right.

From left to right, top to bottom: Evening primrose, *Verbascum bombyciferum*, *Kniphofia* 'Ice Queen', evening primrose, *Hemerocallis* 'Hyperion', *Achillea filipendulina* 'Gold Plate' and gardener's garters.

Achillea filipendulina 'Gold Plate': huge 15cm (6in) plate-like, bright gold flowers on 120cm (4ft) stems mid- to late summer; feathery foliage; herbaceous perennial.
Evening primrose (*Oenothera biennis*): self-seeding biennial growing to 120cm (4ft); masses of large, yellow, single flowers, several gathered towards the tip of each stem, throughout mid-summer.
Gardener's garters (*Phalaris arundinacea* var. *picta*): lime-green and cream-striped evergreen grass; can grow 60–90cm (2–3ft) in good border soil.

Hemerocallis 'Hyperion': scented, wide-open trumpet-flowers of canary yellow over iris-like foliage; mid-summer flowering; 90cm (3ft) high herbaceous perennial.
Kniphofia 'Ice Queen': 1.5m (5ft) high flower spikes of green and cream mid- to late summer; herbaceous/semi-evergreen perennial.
Verbascum bombyciferum: tall (to 1.8m/6ft) architectural biennial with a rosette of huge silver-grey leaves at the base; in mid-summer a succession of pale yellow flowers push their way through the candelabra-like stems which are clad in silvery felt; self-seeding.

An orange colour cameo

A black elder is skirted by (from left to right) *Mimulus cardinalis*, tiger lilies and bronze fennel. *Houttuynia cordata* 'Chameleon' flanks the grass path which leads to a blackberry arch.

Many gardeners find orange, red and yellow difficult to place in the garden as they stand out so strongly from their backgrounds. However, these colours are great fun to play around with if you enjoy the experimental aspect of cottage gardening, and they can produce very striking borders. This orange cameo is a mid- to late summer planting plan which is ideal for soil that stays fairly moist even in summer, and works well in a corner of the garden where you need some height.

Blackberry arch: cultivated blackberries have larger and better fruit than wild ones; 'Oregon Thornless' is suitable for an arch although the flavour is not as good as that of the prickly 'Fantasia'.

Black elder (*Sambucus nigra* 'Purpurea'): bushy, dome-shaped shrub with deep purple leaves which colour best in the sun; in early summer it also has trusses of palest pink flowers which look wonderful set off against the leaves.

Bronze fennel (*Foeniculum vulgare purpureum*): 1.8m (6ft) of delicate feathery bronze foliage topped in summer by flat, yellow flowerheads; birds love their seeds; self-seeding herbaceous perennial.

Houttuynia cordata 'Chameleon': late emerging herbaceous plant with ivy-shaped leaves variegated in yellow, orange and green on stems up to 30cm (1ft) high; insignificant single white flowers in summer; can become invasive on damp ground after a few years; makes a good container plant.

Mimulus cardinalis: striking 60cm (2ft) species with hooded orange flowers; self-seeding hardy annual, flowering mid- to late summer.

Tiger lily (*Lilium lancifolium*, syn. *L. tigrinum*): sensational lily with black spotted, soft orange flowers in late mid-summer; propagate easily from bulbils on stems after flowering; 90–120cm (3–4ft) high.

The potted garden

Potted plants are an essential component of cottage gardens. Traditionally most of them would have been grown on one of the cottage's window sills, but nowadays they are more likely to be grouped informally round the front porch or the back door, or further down the garden, in a collection used to give character and colour to a bench seat. With a collection of different-sized pots by a door, the aim should be to make it look as though the plants are waiting to be planted out. Being portable, potted plants can be moved around when an idea for their positioning strikes you. Meanwhile, you can come up with some unusual plant associations that really work, just by seeing how one plant looks with the other plants by the back door.

Another attractive way of using containers is as the focal point of an enclosed paved area; this effect can be extremely useful. Be sure to include some old-fashioned scented flowers such as scented-leaved pelargoniums, *Nicotiana affinis*, pineapple sage (*Salvia rutilans*), and other aromatic herbs, since the warmth and shelter of an enclosed courtyard area create ideal conditions for perfume to linger. House-leeks (*Sempervivum*), saxifrages, small sedums and other rock plants can be planted in stone troughs.

For an appropriate cottagey look, choose clay flower pots, old stone sinks or animal feeding troughs and other interesting, recycled containers. If you have hanging baskets, choose traditional moss-lined ones instead of the more modern, plastic versions. Make the most of plants growing in pots by grouping them with hanging baskets, at different heights on either side of the door, and use any unusual tall containers you can find.

Compost, feeding and watering

Containers are best filled with a soil-based potting compost, such as John Innes No.3, which will last two to three years before it needs to be replaced, provided the plants are fed regularly. Soilless composts can be used as well, but will need replacing every spring before planting. Garden soil should be avoided as it may harbour pests and diseases.

Stand potted plants on top of the filled container so they can be moved round easily while you decide how best to put them together, then plant by knocking them out of their pots and plunging the rootballs up to their rims in the compost. After planting, water well. Encourage plants to grow bushy and into attractive shapes by 'finger pruning', that is nipping the growing tips of the shoots out between finger and thumb nail in a pincer movement. Remove dead flowerheads regularly and feed with a liquid or soluble plant feed following the manufacturer's recommendation for container-grown plants. Alternatively, use a liquid tomato feed made up at half strength for flowering plants in containers, as the extra potash this contains promotes good flowering. Half-hardy perennial plants must be removed from outdoor containers just before the first frost, potted, and kept on a window sill indoors or in a frost-free greenhouse or sunroom for the winter, unless cuttings have been rooted earlier to use as replacements the following year.

Plants should be checked daily in summer and once a week in winter for watering as the compost in containers does dry out very quickly. The easiest way of checking is to poke your finger a few centimetres

**COTTAGE PLANTS
FOR CONTAINERS**

*Argyranthemum
  foeniculaceum*
*Argyranthemum
  frutescens*
*Argyranthemum
  'Jamaica Primrose'*
Convolvulus tricolor
  cultivars
Datura meteloides
Ivy-leaved pelargoniums
Lemon-scented verbena
Lobelia, trailing
Morning glory
  (*Ipomoea purpurea*)
Nasturtium
  (*Tropaeolum majus*)
Nemophila
Osteospermum
Pineapple sage
  (*Salvia rutilans*)
*Rhodochiton
  atrosanguineus*
Salvia coccinea
Salvia microphylla
  (syn. *S. grahamii*)
Scented-leaved
  pelargoniums
Standard fuchsia
Swan river daisy
  (*Brachycome*)
Tobacco plant
  (*Nicotiana*)
Trailing fuchsia
Upright fuchsia
Zaluzianskya capensis

into the compost to feel if it is moist or dry. Peat-based composts retain more water than other kinds, and terracotta pots dry out faster than plastic pots or those made of non-porous materials.

Putting plants together

When planting containers, or grouping together a collection of potted plants, follow the same general guidelines as when making plant associations for a border (see page 56). Start with a few plants that look good together and add to them, using a mixture of colours, plant shapes and foliage textures for a cottagey look. Vary the pace of the collection: instead of standing everything together, make several well-defined groups of varying heights, each with a definite character of its own. Stand shorter plants with flowing habits, such as *Campanula carpatica* hybrids and baby blue eyes (*Nemophila maculata*) round the outside of a group, to give it a definite edge. And leave taller plants unstaked as far as possible, to lean artistically amongst others in the group. For a place of honour, choose a single, very striking specimen plant, such as *Salvia rutilans*, *S. coccinea* or *S. microphylla* (syn. *S. grahamii*), and put it in an extra special pot in its own space so that it receives the attention it deserves.

For an authentic old-fashioned look, plant your containers with traditional cottage flowers, such as verbenas, zinnias, pelargoniums, fuchsias and nasturtiums, in mixed colours and pastel shades, rather than going for brash new cultivars. Include plenty of daisy-shaped flowers, like *Felicia amygdaloides* and marguerites (*Argyranthemum frutescens*, syn. *Chrysanthemum frutescens*), and varied foliage, and tall plants as well as short. One plant I find specially useful in pots is *Argyranthemum foeniculaceum*; its daisy flowers and glaucous foliage complement all sorts of other plants – I have it with rose campion (*Lychnis coronaria*) and *Solanum laciniatum* (a wickedly poisonous-looking plant with blue potato flowers and vivid green eggs for fruit), growing with a group of potted fruit trees.

This very informal cottage container planting consists of violas and wallflowers (Cheiranthus cheiri) sharing the pot on the brick wall, and a pink rhododendron in the centre, one of the yakushimanum hybrids which are most suited to pot-growing but must be planted in an ericaceous compost. The pot on the right is planted with a mixture of wallflowers and elegant, lily-flowered tulips.

Growing edible crops

No traditional cottage garden would have been without its herbs, fruit and vegetables. More recently, however, edible produce has become a rather neglected part of cottage gardening, largely, I think, in reaction to the old image of a cottage back garden that looked more like an allotment. But the introduction and popularity of colourful and unusual vegetables, and recent developments like fruit trees on dwarfing rootstocks which can be grown very successfully in a small space or even in pots (see page 64), have given rise to a new interest in growing produce for decoration as well as for cooking.

A well-organized vegetable plot, with lots of short rows, will ensure the production of a wider range of different crops in usable quantities. Lettuce, in particular, must be sown little and often to provide continuity of cropping – every two to three weeks throughout the summer is ideal.

Ornamental kitchen gardens

Ornamental kitchen gardens are both productive *and* pleasing to the eye. They are great fun to experiment with and, since most vegetables and a lot of herbs are annuals, you can try out a wide range of different planting plants in a relatively short space of time. In fact, it is desirable to 'rotate' annual crops to a new patch of soil every year to prevent a build-up of soil-borne diseases. A conventional way of doing this is to have one bed for roots including potatoes, one for brassicas and leeks, one for peas and beans, with the fourth for salads and crops like courgettes, rhubarb chard and so on, as illustrated in the planting plan on pages 68–9. However, compared to a traditional cottage kitchen garden, today's ornamental cultivars are not designed to keep you supplied with 'staple' crops, such as maincrop potatoes and onions. Rather, they will give you a little of many different crops, especially the more unusual or interesting varieties.

Due to the closer spacings caused by growing plants in blocks instead of rows, today's vegetables will tend to be smaller than those from traditional plots. But this can be an advantage in the kitchen and a good range of unusual crops are more interesting to cook and to eat than the large quantities of traditional vegetables that a 'real' cottager would have produced. As a general rule, the most attractive crops are coloured versions of common vegetables and salads which are grown in the same way as the more usual coloured crops. You could try red lettuce ('Red Salad Bowl', 'Lollo Rosso') purple-podded beans ('Purple Tepee', a dwarf variety, or the climbing 'Viola Cornetti'), red brussels sprouts ('Rubine') or golden courgettes ('Gold Rush'). There are also more unusual crops such as rhubarb chard, red orache or quinoa, any of which you are likely to need only in small quantities at a time.

Planning the layout

In order to grow a small quantity of lots of different crops, it pays to plan the kitchen garden so that it gives you room for more rows, each of which is shorter than in a conventional kitchen garden (see the planting plan on pages 68–9).

For practicality, as well as good looks, it is best to organize an ornamental kitchen garden on a formal or semi-formal basis, with distinct beds serviced from paths running round the edges. If you are

making beds from scratch, it is a good idea to make them deep, since this is the most productive way of growing vegetables with the close spacings needed in an ornamental garden. Double dig the soil to two spades' depth and fork in lots of well-rotted organic matter, then refill with a mixture of the original soil and more organic matter (see page 36). Make the beds to a width that allows you to work comfortably without stepping on the soil; I find 90cm (3ft) is ideal. Do not tread on the beds when you plant or cultivate as this compacts the soil, making it harder for plant roots to penetrate.

It is a good idea to outline the shape of the ornamental kitchen garden with permanent features, the most appropriate being raspberries, blackberries or other soft fruit. For convenience when pruning or picking, it is advisable to have a path on both sides of these. Perennial vegetables like asparagus are also best serviced from a good path so these should be planted in an outer bed, leaving the main beds free to be changed from one type of crop to another on a

yearly rotation. Anything you will be picking a bit at a time, such as herbs, is best grown as an edging.

One of the secrets of making an ornamental kitchen garden stay ornamental is to avoid having any gaps. You need to know your crops, and have the next batch of young plants ready to go in as soon as the previous crop has been cleared. For example, after summer crops like broad beans have been cleared in late summer, you should be ready with spring cabbage plants for planting in early autumn. Over-wintering vegetables like leeks and sprouts are cleared in spring, when broad bean and lettuce plants can be put in as soon as the ground has been prepared. The best way of ensuring this is to sow seed of crops such as lettuce that can be transplanted in trays, then prick out the best seedlings into 9cm (3½in) pots. You are thus planting out reasonable-sized plants that provide an immediate effect. With crops like beans, seedlings can be left in trays to grow 8–10cm (3–4in) tall before planting out. Root crops must, of course, be sown *in situ*.

The working part of the garden needs to be designed for practicality. Here, an old outbuilding has been converted for use as a toolshed. Beetroot and carrots are planted in short, neat rows; the valerian (Centranthus ruber) beyond screens a pile of old stone, awaiting re-cycling as garden paving.

An ornamental kitchen garden

When planning an ornamental kitchen garden, it is most important to try to achieve a balance between decorative effect and practicality. However pretty the crop, only include what you and your family will actually want to eat. In this plan, staple crops, such as potatoes and roots, are grown to 'fill in' part of the pattern of a formal garden, with more decorative crops forming the central bed. The four beds used for these everyday crops are arranged for convenient rotation. The scheme is illustrated in late mid-summer.

Rotation crops

A Tubers and root crops:
Beetroot
Carrots
Parsnips
Potatoes

B Brassicas and leeks:
Brussels sprouts
Cabbages
Cauliflowers
Leeks
Red kale

C Peas and beans:
Dwarf broad beans
Dwarf french beans
Dwarf peas

D Salad and other crops:
Endive
Garlic
Golden courgettes
Lettuce
Rhubarb chard

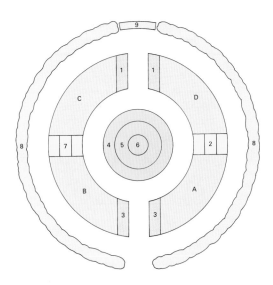

This section of the garden shows, in the foreground, a bed of brassicas and leeks, flanked on the left by runner beans and on the right by jerusalem artichokes. Red orache is planted in the centre with leafless pea and 'Lollo Rosso' lettuce. In the background, beds of peas and beans, and salad and other crops can be glimpsed, separated by an ornamental grape arch and surrounded by soft fruit bushes. The key above shows an aerial view of the whole garden.

1 Asparagus: perennial vegetable with attractive ferny foliage after the asparagus-cutting season which is late spring to early mid-summer. Suggested cultivar: 'Lucullus': an all-male cultivar; female asparagus plants produce inferior spears.

2 Cucumber, outdoor, trained over arches: fruits and flowers throughout the summer; Japanese cultivars are just like greenhouse cucumbers in quality and flavour. Suggested Japanese cultivar: 'Tokyo Cross'.

3 Jerusalem artichoke: 3–3.7m (10–12ft) plants grown annually from tubers planted in spring; strongly resemble bushy sunflowers, flowering in late summer; dig up tubers in late autumn. Suggested cultivars: 'Dwarf Sunray': plant growing 1.5–1.8m (5–6ft); 'Tuscan': long straight tubers which are easier to scrape.

4 Lettuce 'Lollo Rosso': frilly red lettuce which, if left to go to seed, turns into pretty 30cm (1ft) high bronze spirals.

5 Peas, leafless: pretty plant with wiry green tendrils in place of leaves; steam or stir-fry the tendrils as a separate vegetable. Suggested cultivars: 'Twiddy' and 'Markana'.

6 Red orache: coloured version of an ancient vegetable crop; the young leaves can be cut and used like spinach although the flower spikes are more often used in floral arrangements.

7 Runner beans, trained over arches: most forms have red flowers but bi-coloured, white- and pink-flowered cultivars are available; flowering and cropping continue for longer than for climbing french beans although the flavour of the latter is considered superior.

8 Soft fruits, such as blackberry, loganberry and blackcurrant, can be used to edge the vegetable garden (see pages 86–7).

9 *Vitis vinifera* 'Purpurea', trained over an arch: ornamental grape; may yield small purple fruit from late mid-summer.

Growing vegetables

The vegetables included in the ornamental kitchen garden plan on the previous page are all annuals, with the exception of asparagus. Advice on cultivating these vegetables is given below and the chart opposite shows the most suitable sowing, planting and harvesting times for this planting plan. Vegetables can be grown from seed planted directly in the soil, or they can be transplanted after being raised in a greenhouse or seedbed. Alternatively, they can be bought as young plants from a nursery.

Preparing a seedbed

Seedbeds are most convenient situated in a corner of the vegetable garden. Prepare them by digging in organic matter the autumn or winter before sowing. In spring go over the soil with a fork to remove any weeds and break down any clods with a cultivator. This will also remove any small stones and break down the surface of the soil to make a fine tilth. Up to two weeks before sowing, apply a general fertilizer and rake in. After sowing, cover the seed with soil and water in. Vegetables that are sown where they are to crop, such as broad beans, should have their soil prepared in the same way before sowing.

Planting and cultivation

Annual vegetables should be planted in soil that has been prepared by digging in well-rotted organic matter the previous autumn/winter. A fortnight before planting, fork over the soil to remove weeds, sprinkle on a general artificial fertilizer or blood, fish and bone, and rake in. Brassicas should be well firmed in and on no account should they be planted in loose 'fluffy' soil.

After planting, water the vegetables in well and continue watering if the weather is dry. Crops such as courgettes and brussels sprouts that grow clear of the ground can be mulched round with well-rotted organic matter once they have grown enough to ensure their crown of foliage is well above soil level. Supports for climbing beans should be put up before planting the crop. Brussels sprouts are best staked in mid-summer to keep them upright. Feed plants regularly during the growing season, either by liquid feeding or sprinkling general fertilizer over the soil and hoeing and watering in. Do not allow fertilizer to lodge in the leaves as it can cause scorching. Pick vegetables while they are still small and tender. Crops like beans which produce over a long period of time should be picked little and often in order to keep the plants cropping well.

Asparagus should be planted in spring in soil that has been well prepared, by double digging and raking in a general fertilizer. Put the plants in 60cm (2ft) apart in 90cm (3ft) rows, with their crowns 5cm (2in) below the soil surface. Mulch with well-rotted manure and feed regularly every four weeks until mid- to late summer with a liquid feed or by sprinkling general fertilizer round the plants. Asparagus should not be cut for two years to allow plants to establish properly. In the first year of cropping, cut only a few spears; these should be cut 8cm (3in) below ground when they are about 13cm (5in) tall. Stop cutting in early mid-summer to allow the rather attractive fern to develop. This should not be cut down until it yellows naturally in late summer through to autumn. Asparagus plants will last up to 20 years before they need replacing.

ABOVE *The decorative 'pompons' sticking up through the courgette plants are the seed heads of the previous year's crop of leeks which were not all harvested.*

RIGHT *The most suitable sowing, planting and harvesting times for the annual crops in the ornamental kitchen garden plan are given in this chart. The measurements given for planting may vary from cultivar to cultivar. The seasonal bands refer to months which may vary according to the climate in which you live.*

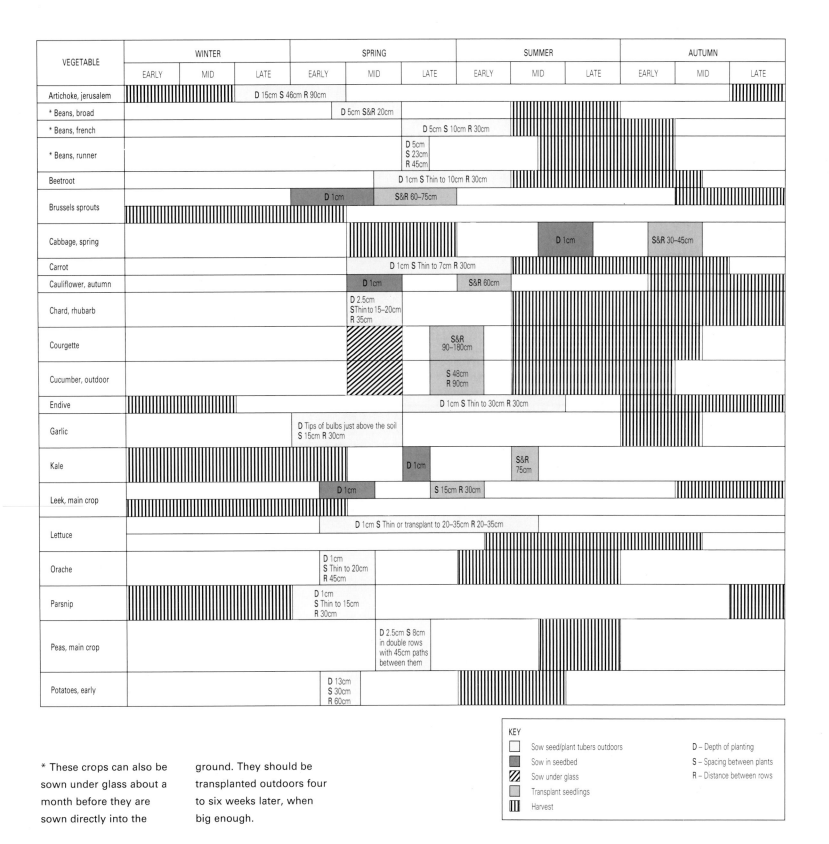

VEGETABLE	WINTER Early	Mid	Late	SPRING Early	Mid	Late	SUMMER Early	Mid	Late	AUTUMN Early	Mid	Late
Artichoke, jerusalem	Harvest	Harvest	Harvest	D 15cm S 46cm R 90cm								Harvest
* Beans, broad						D 5cm S&R 20cm		Harvest				
* Beans, french						D 5cm S 10cm R 30cm		Harvest	Harvest			
* Beans, runner						D 5cm S 23cm R 45cm		Harvest	Harvest			
Beetroot						D 1cm S Thin to 10cm R 30cm	Harvest	Harvest	Harvest	Harvest	Harvest	
Brussels sprouts	Harvest	Harvest		D 1cm	S&R 60–75cm							
Cabbage, spring				Harvest	Harvest			D 1cm		S&R 30–45cm		
Carrot					D 1cm S Thin to 7cm R 30cm		Harvest	Harvest	Harvest	Harvest	Harvest	
Cauliflower, autumn				D 1cm		S&R 60cm				Harvest	Harvest	
Chard, rhubarb				D 2.5cm S Thin to 15–20cm R 35cm			Harvest	Harvest	Harvest	Harvest	Harvest	
Courgette				Sow under glass		S&R 90–180cm	Harvest	Harvest	Harvest	Harvest		
Cucumber, outdoor				Sow under glass		S 48cm R 90cm	Harvest	Harvest	Harvest	Harvest		
Endive	Harvest	Harvest	Harvest			D 1cm S Thin to 30cm R 30cm				Harvest	Harvest	
Garlic				D Tips of bulbs just above the soil S 15cm R 30cm			Harvest	Harvest				
Kale	Harvest	Harvest	Harvest				D 1cm		S&R 75cm			
Leek, main crop	Harvest	Harvest	Harvest	D 1cm		S 15cm R 30cm				Harvest	Harvest	Harvest
Lettuce				D 1cm S Thin or transplant to 20–35cm R 20–35cm			Harvest	Harvest	Harvest	Harvest	Harvest	
Orache				D 1cm S Thin to 20cm R 45cm			Harvest	Harvest	Harvest			
Parsnip	Harvest	Harvest		D 1cm S Thin to 15cm R 30cm							Harvest	Harvest
Peas, main crop						D 2.5cm S 8cm in double rows with 45cm paths between them		Harvest				
Potatoes, early				D 13cm S 30cm R 60cm			Harvest	Harvest				

KEY

- ☐ Sow seed/plant tubers outdoors
- ■ Sow in seedbed
- ▨ Sow under glass
- ▧ Transplant seedlings
- ▥ Harvest

- D – Depth of planting
- S – Spacing between plants
- R – Distance between rows

* These crops can also be sown under glass about a month before they are sown directly into the ground. They should be transplanted outdoors four to six weeks later, when big enough.

A formal herb garden

The plan shown here in mid-summer has a strong base of evergreens and coloured foliage and flowering herbs. This will prevent the herb garden from looking rather bare in winter when the annual herbs are over and overwhelmingly green for the rest of the year. Sufficient quantities of the most useful culinary herbs are included to allow you to cut them for cooking and preserving without spoiling the appearance of the garden.

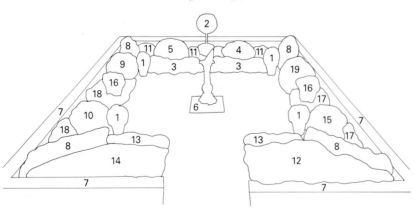

1 Apple mint (*Mentha*): plant all the same mint (as here) or a mixture, such as spearmint, bowles, curly or eau-de-cologne; eau-de-cologne is useful for pot-pourri and excellent for cooking; all are aggressive

spreaders unless contained in large pots; 60–90cm (2–3ft) herbaceous perennials needing annual repotting into rich compost each spring; keep moist.

2 Bay (*Laurus nobilis*): slightly tender

evergreen shrub often trained into pyramids or standard 'lollipop' shapes for growing in pots; makes a big tree if planted out but is controlled easily by pruning when in pots.

3 Chives (*Allium schoenoprasum*): tubular leaves to 30cm (1ft) with mauve spiky flowers in mid-summer; good bee plant; self-seeding herbaceous perennial.

4 Cotton lavender (*Santolina incana*, syn. *S. chamaecyparissus*): 45cm (1½ft) evergreen shrublet with aromatic, silver foliage.

5 Curry plant (*Helichrysum italicum*): slightly tender silver evergreen with narrow leaves and strong curry scent; yellow flowers which appear in mid-summer can be removed if disliked; grows to 60cm (2ft).

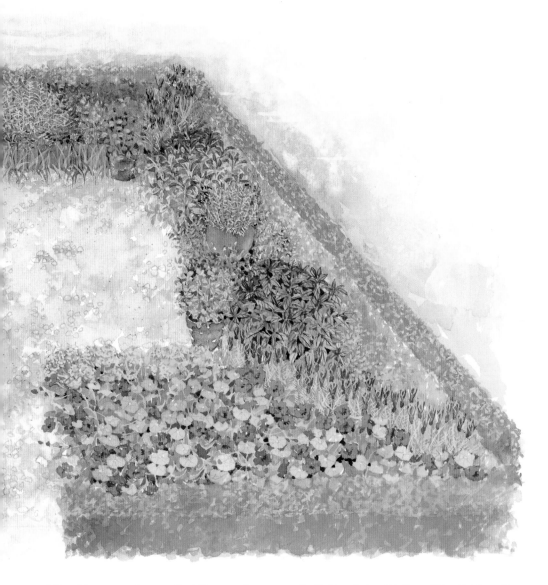

cultivars form a mound to 45cm (1½ft) high; grow compact cultivars if space is short as plants nearby may be smothered; leaves and flowers can be used in salads if you like the hot, peppery taste; hardy annual flowering in summer; sow *in situ* from spring onwards.

13 Parsley (*Petroselinum crispum*): curly-leaved parsley is most decorative in garnishes but plain-leaved parsley is said to taste better; 15cm (6in) biennial grown as an annual; sow *in situ* from early spring.

14 Purple basil (*Ocimum basilicum* 'Dark Opal'): aromatic deep purple foliage which is tastier than the plain green basil; 30cm (1ft) short-lived half-hardy annual; sow seed in pots under glass 3–4 times during the season from early spring onwards and plant out after the last risk of frost.

15 Purple sage (*Salvia officinalis* 'Purpurascens'): edible, purple leaves; 45cm (1½ft) semi-evergreen shrublet.

16 Rosemary (*Rosmarinus officinalis*): slightly tender evergreen shrub with needle-like leaves and blue flowers in early summer; different cultivars are available with upright, prostrate or bushy growth; some even have pink flowers, such as one known simply as pink rosemary (*R. officinalis roseus*).

17 Summer savory (*Satureia hortensis*): little-known herb which deserves more recognition; delicious, mild thyme-like flavour; hardy annual with pink flowers in mid-summer; best sown in pots and planted out when big enough from spring onwards.

18 Thyme (*Thymus* species): wide range of creeping and bushy cultivars available, all evergreen, including culinary thymes – common thyme (*T. vulgaris*), orange thyme (*T. fragrantissimus*) and lemon thyme (*T. citriodora*); height to 30cm (1ft); a mixture of creeping thymes will make a pretty herbal carpet a few centimetres high; flowers different shades of pink in mid-summer.

19 Tricolour sage (*Salvia officinalis* 'Tricolor'): cream, green and pink variegated leaves; 45cm (1½ft) semi-evergreen shrublet.

6 Double roman chamomile (*Chamaemelum nobile* 'Flore Pleno', syn. *Anthemis nobilis* 'Flore Pleno'): scented, feathery leaves and double daisy flowers in mid-summer; 30cm (1ft) mat of foliage; herbaceous perennial.

7 Dwarf box (*Buxus sempervirens* 'Suffruticosa'): very good edging plant which can be clipped back to 8–15cm (3–6in); evergreen shrub.

8 French lavender (*Lavandula stoechas*): good upright grower easily trimmed for low hedges; leaves and flowers (produced in mid-summer) can be used for cooking; slightly tender but can survive the winter if the soil is well-drained; in very cold areas it is best lifted or propagated from cuttings and treated as a half-hardy perennial.

9 Golden balm (*Melissa officinalis* 'Aurea'): 60cm (2ft) herbaceous perennial with golden, lemon-scented foliage; plant on the shady side of a garden as it scorches in hot sun.

10 Gold variegated sage (*Salvia officinalis* 'Icterina'): green and cream leaves; 45cm (1½ft) semi-evergreen shrublet.

11 Knotted marjoram (*Origanum majorana*): also called sweet marjoram and, incorrectly, oregano; the best tasting marjoram for cooking; half-hardy annual growing to 30cm (1ft) with insignificant white flowers produced from 'knotted' buds; sow in pots under glass from early spring onwards for planting out after the last risk of frost.

12 Nasturtium (*Tropaeolum majus*): climbing

LIVING WITH A COTTAGE GARDEN

Once you have created a cottage garden, that is not the end of the story by any means. A cottage garden is not just a hobby; it is more a way of life. Cottage gardens are traditionally intended to be useful as well as ornamental, and whether their function is to provide the raw materials for things you use in the home, or simply to provide a life-long interest — a home for plant enthusiasts to house their treasures and practise the time-honoured art of cultivation — the cottage garden is still fulfilling a useful function today.

Topiary has been used in a most unusual but successful way to dramatize the flowering apple tree behind the yew (Taxus) hedge and to create a distinctive garden boundary. One of the yew plants has been trained into a sphere shape and now nestles beneath the hanging branches of the tree.

Dual-purpose plants

ROSE-HIP SYRUP

Wash, top and tail your rose-hips, and put them in a large heavy saucepan or preserving pan. Just cover with water and boil until soft. 'Mash' with the end of a rolling pin, and stir well until the flesh of the fruit forms a paste. Add a little extra boiling water if the paste is too stiff. Drip through a jelly bag, and then through a bag made from a piece of clean cotton, such as an old pillowcase, to separate the juice. This second 'filtering' is vital to remove all the seeds from the juice as these are extremely irritant. Heat the juice and boil gently until the volume is reduced by about half, then add 570g (1¼lb) sugar to every 850ml (1½ pints) of juice, and boil for another 5 minutes. It will keep in a refrigerator for several weeks, but use sterilized bottles if you wish to store it for longer.

Cottagers in the past relied on the garden to supply many of life's essentials – a pig, poultry and eggs, bees for honey, fruit, vegetables and herbs. From these, cottagers cured hams and bacons and made their own jams, jellies, wine and mead, besides making household goods such as furniture polish from beeswax, and tapers (a poor man's candle, made by dipping the stems of rushes into grease left over after cooking bacon or pork). They also propagated plants from the garden which they would swap with friends, or give to young relatives when they married and started their own home. Many cottage gardeners today still like to grow some of the nostalgic old dual-purpose plants, evocative of the early origins of cottage gardens, such as roses, herbs and fruit trees, whether they actually intend to use them or not. The most important of these are described below, with their uses, and a list of herbs with a household purpose is given on page 99.

Roses

Roses can provide hips for making rose-hip syrup (poured over ice cream, it makes a sensational dessert) and petals for rose petal jelly or wine. The best rose to grow for 'cooking' hips is *Rosa rugosa* and its cultivars such as 'Scabrosa', which has huge, squashed-looking red hips a little like tomatoes in appearance. These are species roses, best grown in a hedge; in order for them to produce hips, they should not be dead-headed. For making wine or jelly, very dark red, highly scented flowers are best. This is a relatively uncommon colour in old-fashioned roses, so it may be worth growing a few 'Papa Meilland' Hybrid Teas specially. Rose petals are also useful for pot-pourri (see page 79).

Herbs

Herbs can be dried for use in winter for flavouring dishes when fresh leaves are not available. Pick them in early summer, well before the plants show any tendency to flower: the easiest way is to cut whole shoots – traditionally this was done in early morning, as people thought herbs lost some of their virtues when the sun had been on them. Swish them round in cold water to remove any dirt or dust, then dip them very briefly into boiling water, as this helps them keep their colour better after drying. Tie up the stems into bunches, but keep them small, otherwise the stems in the middle of the bunch may stay damp and turn mouldy. Then hang the stems upside down in a dust-free place out of direct sun, but where there is a moving current of air; I peg mine to the clothes airer, and leave them in the kitchen with the back door open. When the leaves are crispy-dry, you can easily separate them from the stems by crunching them up between your fingers. Dried herbs store best in dry, airtight glass jars, kept in the dark. Alternatively, you can chop fresh herbs and freeze them in ice-cube trays, adding just enough water to cover them.

Fruit

Most fruit can be made into jams, jellies and home-made wine. But it can be a problem knowing what to do with some of the unusual fruiting trees grown in today's cottage gardens. Medlars, for instance, must be left on the tree as long as possible into the autumn, then picked and stored until they start to go soft and brown (unripe medlars are beige); the inside of the fruit will also be turning brown at this point. They can be eaten raw with cream, though frankly how anyone can is beyond me as they are virtually rotten. I prefer to make them into jelly, which is surprisingly tasty, and is used in much the same way as redcurrant jelly, as an accompaniment to meat – medlar jelly is also nice mixed with equal quantities of crab apple jelly, to serve with turkey or game.

Crab apples are picked in autumn, just before they start to fall naturally, and made into wine or jelly. 'John Downie' is the best jellying cultivar as the hips are a good size and have a pretty rosy colour which comes through in the finished product. It makes the best jelly I have ever tasted.

HERB JELLY

Follow your favourite recipe for apple jelly, but add finely chopped fresh herbs before starting to boil or add whole herb leaves tied up in a muslin bag, to be removed when the jelly is strained. Vary the quantity according to taste, to give a mild or strong herby flavour. The best herbs to use as 'individual' herb jellies include mint, thyme, and sage, but you could also experiment with various mixtures of herbs, and some of the scented-leaved geraniums are also good used in this way.

Mulberries make attractive specimen trees. If you buy a grafted plant of a named variety, such as 'Chelsea', you can be picking fruit from it within two to three years, instead of the ten or so you would otherwise have to wait. The fruits ripen in mid-summer and look like blackish-purple raspberries growing from the twigs. Mulberries are traditionally gathered by laying old sheets under the branches and simply waiting for them to fall. They have a most delicious, sweet taste and can be eaten fresh with cream, or made into jam, wine or pies.

Quince should be left on the tree as long as possible, but picked before the weather starts to deteriorate in autumn. Lay them out in a shed or cool spare bedroom until they turn golden, when they are ready to use (ripe quince are beautifully scented). They make a good wine, or can be peeled and cored and added to apple pies, for flavouring.

Quince (Cydonia oblonga) makes an attractively shaped small tree which gnarls naturally with age. It provides spring blossom, followed by fruit that is both ornamental and edible, and persists on the tree well into the autumn.

Flowers for drying

Edible plants were not the only useful ones grown in cottage gardens. A lot of flowering plants are dual-purpose too. The traditional thrift of cottagers would have made cutting flowers simply to display in a vase seem wasteful. They would have preferred to grow flowers and then dry them so they could be kept longer. The flowers that dry well look quite at home in a cottage garden; they are among the few annuals that we make room for.

To pick flowers for drying, you need to cut them when the flowers have only just opened. In the case of everlasting flowers, one of the best known being *Helichrysum*, cut them while they are still in bud, as the flowers continue opening for several days after they are cut, even though they are out of water, and can end up past their best if you leave it too late. As with herbs, early morning is the traditional time to cut for drying, but avoid picking them before the dew on them has dried. Once picked, hang them up in small bunches, just like herbs, in a cool, airy place out of direct sun. Some flowers take longer to dry than others, but once they are stiff you can turn them back up the right way, untie the bunches, and stand them in large, empty jars. This spaces the flowers further apart, and there is more air passing between them to complete the drying process. Do not try to dry the flowers initially in an upright position, as the heads may droop as the stems dry out. *Helichrysum* heads are usually removed from their stems and fixed to florist's wires. If left on their natural stems, they will droop and may even fall off completely.

Seedheads such as love-in-a-mist (*Nigella*) and poppy (*Papaver*) should be picked while they are still green, after the stems have started to harden but before they start to dry out naturally, otherwise they tend to fade. Stand plants with stiff stems in jars in a cool, airy place out of sunlight to dry; plants with weak stems should be hung upside down to dry.

Once completely dry, seedheads and dried flowers can be stored in a spare bedroom or a cupboard where they will not get dusty – ideally, upright in jars with the heads spaced out – until you want to use them. They can then simply be put into large vases or jugs or arranged in the special flower-arranging foam sold especially for dried flowers. If you later get tired of the arrangement, you can always take it apart and re-use the same flowers in a different way. In a disused fireplace, dried flowers look attractive arranged with a pile of stored pumpkins and gourds. You can even mix dried flowers with fresh ones; the base of the

FLOWERS AND SEEDHEADS FOR DRYING

Flowers
Bells of ireland
  (*Moluccella laevis*)
Craspedia globosa
Everlasting flower
  (*Helichrysum*)
Globe amaranth
  (*Gomphrena globosa*)
Hydrangea
Lady's mantle
  (*Alchemilla mollis*)
Matricaria
Statice (*Limonium*)
Straw flower
  (*Helipterum*)
Yarrow (*Achillea*)

Seedheads
Bulrushes (reedmace)
Love-in-a-mist (*Nigella*)
Ornamental grasses
  such as quaking grass
  (*Briza maxima*)
Poppy (*Papaver*)
Reeds such as
  Phragmites
Scabious
  (*Scabiosa stellata*)
Teasel (*Dipsacus
  fullonum sylvestris*)

stems rot after a while, but they can be cut shorter and used again. Both dried flowers and seedheads can be picked from their stems and used in collages or pot-pourri. After a year or so, dried flowers get dusty and the colours start to fade, and at this stage they are best thrown out and replaced with new ones.

Pot-pourri

Pot-pourri has been used for many centuries as a natural 'air freshener'. It is a mixture of different kinds of dried flower petals, leaves and small whole dried flowers, and sometimes other ingredients such as twists of dried orange peel, pieces of bark, small fir cones and spices. The mix can be varied according to the scent and the appearance you want to create. Pot-pourri looks pretty in a lidded glass jar, and this is the best way of using it in a room with damp air, like a bathroom, but you only get the benefit of its scent if it is spread out in open, shallow bowls.

The flower petals, whole flowers and orange peel are dried by spreading them out, one layer deep, on a tray or newspaper, and leaving them in a cool, dark, airy place. When they are completely dry they can be stored in airtight glass jars until you are ready to use them. Roses are particularly good flowers to use for pot-pourri; reds and mauves keep their colour best when the petals are dried but white and yellow rose petals tend to go brown.

Powdered orris root is normally added to help 'fix' the scent. It is available from herbalists but can be made at home by drying and grating the roots of *Iris* 'Florentina'. The amount used depends on the extent to which you want the perfume of the orris to dominate – use anything from a teaspoonful to 100g (4oz) per pudding basin of pot-pourri. After a few months, the natural scent of pot-pourri starts to fade but it is easily refreshed by sprinkling on a few drops of aromatic oil, such as rose or ylang-ylang.

FLOWERS FOR
POT-POURRI
Petals
Clove carnation
Lavender
Marigold
Pinks
Rose

Whole flowerheads
Gypsophila
Everlasting flower
Rosebuds

Leaves
Bay
Bergamot
Lavender
Lemon balm
Lemon verbena
Marjoram
Mint (especially the
   eau-de-cologne variety)
Rose
Rosemary
Sage
Scented-leaved
   pelargonium
Thyme

Spices
Cinnamon sticks
Cloves
Coriander seeds
Juniper berries, dried
Nutmegs

LEFT *Roses are best dried before they have opened fully, using silica gel crystals. The crystals must cover the whole flower and be worked in carefully between the layers of petals.*

RIGHT *Small posies of dried lavender can be used in baskets as decorations, or added to pot-pourri. Lavender bags were traditionally tucked into drawers of linen to perfume it.*

The evolving garden

Iris pallida 'Variegata' combines attractively with yellow musk (Mimulus) to soften the edge of this waterlily pond.

Before long, you find yourself wanting to make more drastic changes, like converting what was once just rough grass to a flowering meadow, or developing a theme garden where you can experiment with particular colour schemes or types of plants. Once the children have grown up and left home, and you no longer need so much grass, what could be more logical than to widen the borders to make room for all the extra plants you have always wanted to grow? As soon as you have more time on your hands, the garden is a natural place in which to spend it.

Making the changes

Some people, knowing that they will want to alter the garden in a major way when the family has grown up, deliberately plan with that in mind. The framework of the garden – permanent features like hedges, internal partitions, and specimen trees – are placed in such a way that the detail round them can be altered, leaving the basic shape of the garden intact. The planting can then be developed, becoming much more detailed as new features are added.

The plan on the opposite page shows how the garden on page 51 could look after a few years of further development. A pond and wild flower corner have replaced the original herb garden, and the vegetable patch has been developed into an ornamental kitchen garden, screened by blackberry bushes. A glass-sided garden room extension has been built out over part of the paved area at the rear of the house for tender perennials, and a theme garden (see page 60) has been created in what was part of the large border. The theme could vary over the years as interests change, perhaps from a white garden to a herb garden, then possibly a scented garden. The lawn has now been reduced, and a new path has been cut through the carpet of spreading plants at the end of the garden. The 'Jekyll' border opposite the garden room is a bit of fun, and uses a gradually changing sequence of colour across the border, starting with blue at one end and purple at the other, with yellow, orange and red in the middle.

One thing every keen cottage gardener will tell you is that their garden is never finished. It is the nature of today's cottage garden to be constantly changing. No sooner have you finished planting the basic garden than improvements start springing to mind. You might begin by moving a few plants around to create more pleasing plant associations. You may go on to add an arch here or extend a border there.

Developing the garden

Although the backbone planting of trees and hedges has been retained, this garden bears little resemblance to how it appeared when first planted (see below and page 51).

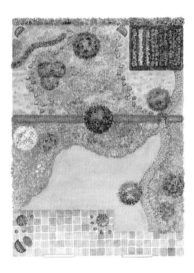

1 *Wild flowers*
2 *Pond*
3 *Bower made of rustic poles*
4 *Ornamental kitchen garden*
5 *Blackberry bushes*
6 *Wild flower lawn*
7 *Fruit trees*
8 *Rose arch*
9 *Rambling roses climbing up pillars*
10 *Herb border*
11 *Theme garden*
12 *Cottage border*
13 *Topiary*
14 *'Jekyll' border*

Topiary

SUITABLE PLANTS
FOR SIMPLE
TOPIARY SHAPES
Bay (Laurus nobilis)
Box (Buxus
    sempervirens)
Chamaecyparis lawsoniana
    'Fletcheri'
Cupressus elwoodii
Holly (Ilex aquifolium)
Privet (Ligustrum
    ovalifolium)
Yew (Taxus baccata)

Topiary is not an authentic cottage garden art. It originally featured in much grander establishments, since large country houses were the only places where anyone had the time to tend such elaborate creations – especially in the days when hedges were cut by hand, using shears. But photographs of nineteenth- and early twentieth-century cottage gardens often show formally clipped hollies growing up through the hedges, trimmed into neat lollipops or mushroom shapes (they cannot have been particularly easy to look after, as many of them were 5m/16ft or so high). But in comparatively recent years the country house style of topiary has slowly crept into cottage gardens. I recently saw a country cottage whose entire front garden was filled by a splendid yew peacock, set off by neatly clipped lengths of formal yew hedge to make a background. Other than the time needed to clip the peacock to shape two or three times a year, the garden probably involved no more hours of work than the weeding and tidying of a conventional cottage flower border.

Old cottage gardens were an odd blend of informal and formal features – remember all those rigid rows of plants along the edges of paths – so topiary does not look at odds in a cottagey flower garden, and can play a variety of roles within it. A solid topiary shape can be a useful way of creating a sharp bend in a path, concealing a new style of planting beyond. It can make an interesting feature in a lawn, or by a corner of the cottage. And a row of small but similar topiary shapes contrasts well with surrounding flowers. One garden I know has a row of 45cm (1½ft) high box spheres running along the edge of a cottagey border; the effect is to provide a visual link between a lot of violently different shapes and colours. In another garden, a row of *Chamaecyparis lawsoniana* 'Fletcheri', clipped into low candle-flame shapes, lines a path planted entirely with shades of green. This leads from one highly colourful area of the garden to another, giving the eye a much needed rest *en route*. Small, formal topiary shapes are also an appropriate way of finishing off a formal herb garden: try adding decorative knobs to the corners of low hedges, and pyramids or lollipop shapes within the design – these help to keep the shape of the garden in winter when the herbs have died down.

Training topiary

Proper topiary takes years to train. Large or complicated shapes are supported from within by a metal frame which is placed over the tree when it is young,

Making a topiary sphere

Use a plastic-covered wire netting frame as the plastic will prevent the wire from rusting. The frame should be fastened firmly to a metal post that has been driven into the ground close to one side of the parent plant. Train in the new growths to the wire until it is covered with foliage. Small-leaved, slow-growing plants like box and yew are most suitable for complicated topiary shapes, such as illustrated here.

Make a sphere shape out of wire and fix securely to the post protruding through the hedge.

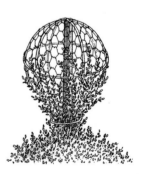

Tie in new growth to the frame. Clip short any side shoots to encourage branching.

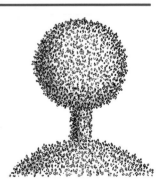

Once formed, the topiary will need clipping only once or twice a year to keep it neat and tidy.

These sharply contrasting topiary shapes show how far eccentricity can be taken in the cottage garden. Topiary really can be trained into whatever shape you choose.

shape it most closely resembles in its natural form, such as a squirrel, or a top hat, then just keep clipping it to reinforce that shape. Solid block shapes like pillars are quite easy to grow in this way; once roughly formed, you can cut spirals around upright spire shapes. You can give an established conifer hedge a castellated top by cutting out square shapes every 45cm (1½ft) or so; you can even cut 'peep-holes' in it, using the surrounding frame of foliage to accentuate a distant view. With more elaborate small shapes, like animals or solid spheres, created on top of existing simple topiary shapes such as a pillar, you can cheat by making the shape in wire netting (see the illustration on the left).

While shapes are being formed, it is a good idea to clip even slow-growing species at least four times a year – each time you cut, you effectively remove the growing tips of the shoots and encourage side-shoots to develop, which thicken the growth and help make the shape. Clip progressively less hard on each occasion to allow the shape to fill out, while still keeping its outline. This way a dense network of shoots will build up. Once formed, the shape then needs clipping only once or twice a year, provided a slow-growing shrub like yew or holly has been used. It is wise to avoid fast-growing shrubs, like ever-green *Lonicera nitida*, which need very frequent cutting to retain the desired shape.

Topiary in pots

You can use the same principal to grow topiary trees in pots. Bay or box can be grown into pyramids or lollipops, for instance. It is fun to dot these round wherever you fancy them, by the front door, or beside a seat for instance. It is vital to keep container-grown topiary well watered; browning topiary looks dreadful, and if it dies you have wasted a lot of time and work. An even faster way of creating your own topiary is to grow climbers such as ivy over a pre-formed shape (which can now even be bought ready-made for this purpose), giving you almost instant results.

before training begins, and left in place as the tree grows, to be hidden by the dense growth of foliage. The bush should be allowed to grow reasonably naturally, encouraged by light trimming to take on a simple shape such as a cube or a cone. When it is big enough, individual shoots can be allowed to grow up through the top for about 60cm (2ft). These are then wired together in loose bunches or tied to canes to start forming, for instance, the shape of a crown or the fan of a peacock's tail. As side-shoots grow out from the framework stems, these are lightly but frequently clipped to make them sprout more side-shoots, so the shape is gradually clad with foliage.

The traditional cottage garden method aims to keep topiary simple. Here, you start with a young bush such as yew, scrutinize it, and imagine the

Tree fruits

Standard trees, or half-standards, are the most traditional shape of fruit tree in the cottage garden. Grafted on a semi-dwarfing or even more dwarfing rootstock (see below), you will have a tree that looks the part with its spreading branches but that will not get too big. Trees on dwarfing rootstocks are also quicker to start cropping; you will be picking fruit within a few years instead of the ten or so that would be the case with more vigorous rootstocks.

Standard and half-standard trees
A standard tree has a trunk 1.5–2.2m (5–7ft) high, topped by a crown of branches; technically, trees with shorter trunks, 90cm–1.5m (3–5ft) high, are called half-standards.

Bush tree
This is simply a standard tree with an even shorter trunk, 75–90cm (2½–3ft) high, giving a bushy appearance. If a bush fruit tree is growing in grass, make sure the lowest branches are high enough to allow a lawnmower to go underneath comfortably.

Rootstocks
In the past, fruit trees were grown on rootstocks that allowed them to grow into large trees but were slow to start cropping. Nowadays, newer rootstocks result in trees that grow to a certain size and then virtually stop, although the ultimate size is also dependent on the quality of soil and growing conditions generally. For poor soil, choose a rootstock one step less dwarfing than you would for good soil. As a general rule, the more dwarfing the rootstock the smaller the ultimate size of the tree and the less it will yield.

The most useful dwarfing rootstocks for cottage garden apple trees are M26 and MM106, which will need staking for the first few years. M26 gives a tree about 3m (10ft) tall which grows well in normal soil conditions, fruiting in three to four years. This rootstock is ideal for stronger growing apple cultivars, and can also be used for trees in pots. MM106 is suitable for weaker growing cultivars, poorer soils, and also for growing in pots. Trees grow to 4.5m (15ft) and start to crop in three to four years.

Moderately dwarfing rootstocks such as these, rather than very dwarfing ones, should be chosen for trees grown in large pots (38–45cm/15–18in) as the pot restricts the tree size naturally by confining its roots. Apples and pears are the most suitable types of tree fruit for containers, although figs are ideal for growing in pots since they need their roots restricted to make them more productive.

Formative pruning of a bush tree

Prune the main stem back to about 75cm (2½ft) to a strong lateral, ensuring there are three to four well-placed laterals beneath it. Remove any other branches flush with the stem (see 1, right). The following year, cut the laterals back by one third or one half (see 2, right). In the third year after planting, cut back the one or two shoots that have grown from near the tips of the original three or four branches by about half (see 3, right).

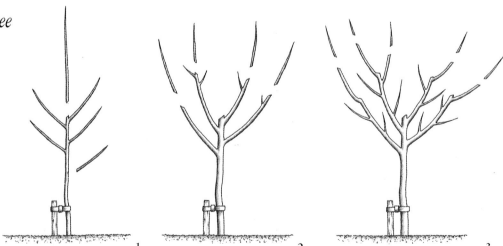

1   2   3

Growing conditions

Fruit trees do best in deep fertile soil and a reasonably sheltered, sunny situation. They are best planted when dormant, that is between leaf fall in autumn and bud break in early spring, avoiding times when the ground is very wet, frozen or muddy, or during drought. Bare-rooted fruit trees (and bushes) dug up from a nursery bed are a good buy. They are available only in the dormant season and should be planted immediately, provided the ground is suitable. Before planting, dig in plenty of well-rotted garden compost or animal manure, then make a large enough planting hole to allow you to spread the roots out well, making sure that the old soil mark on the trunk is level with the soil surface. If you buy container-grown plants, these can be planted in the garden during the growing season. They should be knocked out of their pots with minimal root disturbance (except where roots are tightly packed in their pots, in which case a few of the largest should be gently teased out) and planted in soil prepared with plenty of organic matter and kept well watered for the rest of the season.

Fruit trees for growing in pots should be planted during the dormant season in a soil-based compost, such as John Innes No.3, with 2.5cm (1in) of coarse gravel in the bottom of the pot for drainage. Water whenever the compost is dry – in summer twice daily watering may be necessary. Feed every fortnight during the growing season with general purpose liquid feed. Every two or three years, before growth resumes in spring, take the trees from their pots, remove the compost and trim the roots slightly. Re-pot in fresh compost in the same container.

Pruning and training

Pruning is not absolutely essential for apple and pear trees trained into bush, standard and half-standard shapes, although it is a good idea to thin out excess growth to allow light and air into the middle of the tree. This improves the fruit size and colour, and reduces the risk of disease. Dead, damaged or diseased shoots should always be removed right back to healthy growth. The pruning of these three shapes is essentially the same. All will need staking for the first four or five years.

Pruning should always take place during the dormant season when there are no leaves on the tree. If you are starting with a young 'maiden' tree that has not already been trained by the nursery, the main stem should be pruned back to the height required for the trunk of the tree immediately after planting. Make sure there are three to four suitably placed laterals just beneath the cut (see the illustration on the left). (If you are training a tall standard tree, you may need to allow the tree to grow without pruning for a year or two until the main stem reaches the necessary height.) The following winter, start pruning to form the 'crown' of the tree. Cut back the three or four laterals that radiate out all round at the top of the trunk by one third or one half to encourage sideshoots to grow the following spring (see the illustration on the left). Remove any other branches flush with the main stem.

The third winter after planting, identify the one or two strong shoots that have grown from near the tips of the three or four original branches and cut each of these back by about half (see the illustration on the left). These give a 'second stage' of branching which helps build up the framework of the tree shape. Leave all the other sideshoots that have grown from the original three or four main branches unpruned. The pruning of young trees that have already been trained by the nursery should begin at this third stage.

The following winter and thereafter, little pruning is needed. Broken, damaged or diseased shoots should be cut back to an outward facing bud where the wood is healthy or at a junction with another shoot. Any shoots that are too long or spoil the shape of the tree can be shortened by about half, cutting to just above a growth bud. Shoots growing into the centre of the tree, which would cause overcrowding, should be removed entirely or shortened to 10cm (4in) to create a 'spur' which will carry fruit without taking up much room.

'Ashmead's Kernel'
The exact parentage of this very old eating apple is unknown although it is thought to have originated in Gloucestershire before 1700. Like many old apples, it probably developed by chance, from a pip, and was then propagated because the fruit was so delicious. Old apples are often very small – not much bigger than crab apples – and 'Ashmead's Kernel' certainly has small fruit in comparison with modern cultivars. Greenish yellow with a brown flush on the sunny side, this apple has survived mainly because of the lovely flavour of the rich, juicy, yellow flesh. Like many older apples, it keeps well – it is not properly ripe until mid-winter and lasts until spring, given good storage conditions.

Soft fruits

Soft fruits are often overlooked in modern cottage gardens due to lack of space, but trained fruit bushes and cane fruits look attractive and need not take up much room. The main ways of training soft fruit are summarized below. Growing your own soft fruit gives a pleasant feeling of self-sufficiency. You can grow cultivars selected for fruit quality and flavour rather than high yields, and really enjoy the experience of fruit picked at the peak of perfection. Most soft fruits will produce a light crop in their second year and be in full production by year three. The growing conditions required for soft fruits are the same as for tree fruits (see page 85).

Plants put in during the winter should be pruned hard after planting; if planted in summer the nursery will have pruned during the previous winter and nothing further is necessary until the following winter. In spring, feed soft fruit by sprinkling general fertilizer such as blood, fish and bone and spread a thick mulch of well-rotted organic matter round the plants, taking care that it does not touch the stems. I like to feed again with sulphate of potash just after picking, but this is not essential. A second mulch can also be given in autumn, if required – it is particularly beneficial to plants growing in light soils or if weeds are a problem (see page 38).

Pruning fruit bushes

Fruit bushes, such as blackcurrants, redcurrants and gooseberries, grow naturally into a bushy shape without any special training. Pruning is advisable since old fruited branches need to be removed periodically to keep the plants productive. You should also remove branches that grow into the centre of the bush and thin out the surrounding shoots to allow light in, to help prevent disease, and to make picking easier. Blackcurrants fruit best on one-year old wood while redcurrants and gooseberries fruit on two- and three-year-old wood.

For blackcurrants planted in winter, cut the whole plant down to 8cm (3in) above ground level. No major pruning is needed for the following two winters, except to cut out to ground level any very weak, damaged, out-of-shape or congested shoots. If you plant during the summer, start pruning the following winter. Plants start cropping lightly the second summer after planting.

By the fourth winter, blackcurrant plants are a thick cluster of shoots of various ages; the oldest shoots are heavily branched while the youngest are straight and unbranching. Prune to remove the oldest branches to ground level, or to a junction with a strong young shoot low down in the bush – this encourages productive young branches to take the place of older ones. Avoid removing more than one third of the volume of the bush in any one year.

Redcurrants and gooseberries are grown on a 15cm (6in) high 'leg' – a short trunk with branches radiating out from the top, unlike blackcurrants where new shoots arise directly from the soil (see below). Plant them in winter and cut back the main branches by half; for redcurrants cut to an outward facing bud, but since gooseberry branches invariably droop, cut to an upward pointing bud to try and keep the plant as upright as possible. Cut off flush any branches growing out from the 'leg'.

The following winter, all the current year's growth at the tips of the shoots should be shortened by half. This new growth is recognizable as the bark is a lighter colour. Again, remove completely any

Growing habits of fruit bushes

Redcurrants and gooseberries

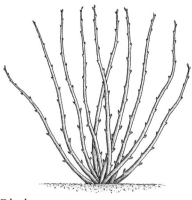

Blackcurrants

shoots arising from the 'leg' of the plant. From then on it is advisable to prune in both summer and winter. In mid-summer, nip back the tips of all the sideshoots to just above the point where the fruit has formed. In winter, cut back the current year's growth by half, and remove any dead or broken branches back to the junction with a sound one.

Growing cane fruit

Blackberries and loganberries fruit on long, twining stems produced the previous summer. These can be trained out horizontally along a fence, up over a garden arch or along a post-and-wire framework. The one-way system, more suitable for a large garden as it takes up a lot of space, is illustrated below. If space is limited, the branches can be concertinaed together, as in the weaving system (see below), which is best suited to thornless cultivars.

Blackberries and loganberries should be planted 3–4.5m (10–15ft) apart in winter and cut back to 25cm (10in) above ground. No pruning is needed during the first year. In year two, keep the new canes separate from those of the previous year as the latter will carry the crop. New canes can be bunched loosely together, or trained out to the opposite side of the support framework from the cropping canes.

After picking, the old canes which carried the crop are cut down to 10–15cm (4–6in) above ground level, and the young canes which have grown during the current year are tied into their place. Plants start cropping the second summer after planting.

Summer-fruiting raspberries should be planted in winter, 45cm (1½ft) apart in rows. Cut all the stems down to just above a bud about 23cm (9in) above ground level. The following year, tie new shoots in as they grow, 10–15cm (4–6in) apart, to a post-and-wire framework – the top wire should be about 1.8m (6ft) high. New plants will fruit in their second year. After picking, cut all fruited canes down to ground level and tie in the new canes; these can be recognized by their lighter coloured stems and lack of sideshoots. Prune weak or overcrowded new stems to ground level. Autumn-fruiting raspberries should also be planted in winter, and cut down to 10cm (4in) above ground level in early spring. Canes only need support if they are very vigorous. They are shorter than summer-fruiting kinds and can be grown in small blocks rather than rows if more convenient. After picking is finished, leave the old stems which should not be pruned until early spring when they are *all* cut down to ground level. Plants start cropping the autumn after planting.

Training blackberries

One-way system: After harvesting, cut down the fruited canes to ground level. Train new canes along the wires in the opposite direction to the previous year's growth (see 1, right). Weaving system: Tie in the first year canes to left and right, weaving them in and out of the bottom three wires. The following year, train the new canes through the centre of the bush and tie them to the top wire (see 2, right). After harvesting, cut the fruited canes down to ground level, untie the remaining canes and weave them in to either side.

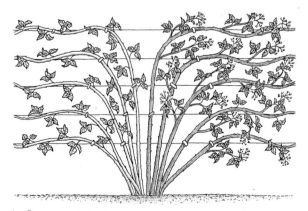

1 *One-way system*

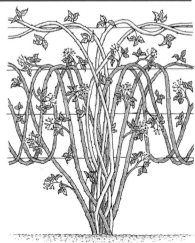

2 *Weaving system*

Antique fruit and vegetables

If you want to add an unusual touch of authenticity to a cottage garden, why not try growing the varieties of fruit and vegetables that were cultivated in the past? There is now a growing interest in 'vintage' varieties, and plants and seeds can be obtained for those still in existence from specialist seed firms and fruit nurseries. In the UK, The National Centre for Organic Gardening runs a heritage seed library from which members can draw a few packets of seed per year; in the US, the Seed-Savers' Exchange helps enthusiasts to save and swap seeds.

Old varieties often turn out to be great finds, with a wonderful flavour and fascinating appearance, even if they do not always crop quite as heavily as modern ones. Both old fruit and vegetables are cultivated in exactly the same way as modern varieties, though they are specially suitable for growing organically because they were developed before the advent of artificial fertilizers, when natural feeds and organic matter were all that was available.

Old fruit

Some of the old varieties of fruit have problems that new varieties have sought to improve on, such as susceptibility to disease, slowness in cropping, irregular or light crops.

Part of the charm of very old fruit trees in cottage gardens is the way they grow gnarled and misshapen. This may be partly due to lack of remedial pruning early on but it is also due to the fact that many old varieties are generally more susceptible to canker than modern ones and this can distort the habit of growth. Canker is a fungal disease causing lesions on the bark of trunks and stems which eventually dies and breaks away. There is no cure other than to prune the affected parts out but this is not always practical. Much of the scarring and general weather-beaten appearance of old apple trees is caused by canker. The eating apple 'Kentish Fillbasket', dating back to pre-1820, gets a lot of canker and cures itself, leading to all sorts of lumps and bumps, as does the cooking apple 'Catshead' (pre-1600). Many other old apples still in existence have this knack of curing their own cankers, which is how they have been able to survive so long. The modern eating apple 'Spartan' and the wild hedge crab apple (*Malus sylvestris*) are also good 'gnarlers'.

Some varieties of fruit, such as victoria plums and many old apples, have the habit of bearing enormous crops one year, followed by one or sometimes two years when they have little or no crop – hence the term 'biennial bearer'. The fact that biennial bearers would have been allowed to carry over-heavy crops which dragged the branches down also resulted in misshapen trees. This accounts for the charming 'props' you often see holding up drooping branches of old apple trees in cottage gardens. You can, however, prune even modern trees to give them an authentic lopsided appearance, or 'train' them by holding young branches down with wire for a year or two to re-create the look of an old cottage garden tree. You could also choose a tree such as a weeping mulberry or medlar which will give an interesting shape without any pruning or training.

It is often worth putting up with the minor defects of old varieties of fruit for what cottage gardeners consider their superior flavour. If you buy trees grafted on to dwarfing rootstocks, they will start cropping sooner than traditional standard trees (see page 84). The smaller trees also take up less room, so you can plant a wider range of varieties – that way, if one or two varieties are having 'off' years, the rest will make up for it. I grow a complete orchard of old apple and pear varieties in large pots, trained as upright cordons. They are grown on moderately dwarfing, rather than very dwarfing, rootstocks such as M26 and MM106, as the pot restricts the roots and keeps the plants small – on extremely dwarfing rootstocks they would hardly grow at all. Pot-grown fruit trees need a lot of watering in summer, but can turn a path or paved area into a productive and colourful feature, and provide a little of several different varieties to try. Opposite are some of my favourite old varieties, most of which can be grown in pots or in the soil.

A part of this back garden is screened from the house by an old apple tree, whose branches have been trained out almost horizontally. It takes up very little room and casts much less shade than a standard tree. The lattice-like pattern of the branches forms natural peepholes which frame tiny cameos of the cottage and garden beyond.

Apples

'Ashmead's Kernel': a 300-year-old eating apple with crisp yellow flesh and an outstanding flavour; one of the best old apples still available. A light, irregular cropper, it needs a well-sheltered situation and a mild climate to do well. Store fruit to use from mid-winter to spring.

'Blenheim Orange': a 200-year-old dual-purpose variety, best eaten straight from the tree in early autumn, then used for cooking until mid-winter; it becomes a bit insipid for eating if kept.

'Bramley's Seedling': discovered in 1809, grown from a pip, this has been *the* cottage-garden cooking apple tree ever since; the shape is naturally spreading and becomes well-gnarled with age and the apples are well-flavoured, with a good, firm texture.

'Irish Peach': Irish variety dating back to 1820; now scarce, but incredibly delicious, juicy fruit best eaten straight from the tree in late summer; the light green fruit is shaded with peach.

'Ribston Pippin': discovered before 1700; aromatic eating apples with an outstanding flavour, like Cox's 'Orange Pippin' but better (it is one of the parents of Cox); a light cropper.

Pears

'Doyenne du Comice': from France, 1849; produces sensational, aromatic, juicy pears but is an unreliable cropper and needs a very warm, sheltered spot in order for it to fruit well.

'Seckle': small, red-tinged fruit that ripen in mid-autumn but stay in good condition for only a few days; delicious buttery flavour with a hint of honey and a musky scent. Needs a warm, sheltered location; date of first appearance unknown.

'William's Bon Chrétien': another tasty, juicy, aromatic pear that dates from 1770. It needs a warm location to crop well, and the fruit do not store well.

Other tree fruit

Greengage – 'Old Green Gage': an ancient fruit of unknown origins; gives a good crop about one year in four, but these are superb-tasting fruit eaten straight from the tree as they ripen; not suitable for pots as adequately dwarfing rootstocks are unavailable.

Plum – 'Victoria': dates from 1840; yellow-red plums that still cannot be beaten for flavour, even though the trees only crop well in alternate years at best; not suitable for pots, as above.

Old vegetables

Old varieties of vegetables are well suited to organic growing, as this would have been the only form of cultivation at the time they were developed. They grow specially well in deep beds (see page 67). Today, they can out-perform modern hybrids when grown organically, as the latter are bred for cultivation in 'optimum' growing conditions – which means soils that are fed regularly with artificial fertilizers. Old varieties are often more useful to the cottage gardener, as they were generally bred to produce crops over a long period of time – unlike modern varieties, many of which have been bred to crop all at the same time.

Saving seeds

Seeds of old open-pollinated vegetable varieties are cheaper to buy than many modern cultivars – often costing less than half the price for more than two or three times the amount of seed in a packet. Open-pollinated means not a hybrid, so by growing open-pollinated vegetables, it is possible to save your own seed and the resulting plants will come true, provided they are not accidentally crossed with a similar plant of another variety growing nearby. When you are saving seed, it is important to leave a few pods or flowers on the plants to set seed, then collect the seed pods or cases once they have dried out naturally. The seeds should be emptied into paper envelopes for storage; plastic or sealed drums are unsuitable, especially for bean seeds, as fungal activity in such containers may prevent germination. The original cottagers would always have saved seeds, although new varieties would occasionally have been acquired from outside the area or from one of the gardeners working at the local 'big house'. Today, saving seed at home is often the only way some old varieties are kept in cultivation, once they cease to be listed by seed firms.

Recommended vegetables

Artichokes are one example of the sort of romantic, pretty vegetable the Victorian and Edwardian artistic cottage gardener would have grown with flowers. Skirret, though less well known, would have

been used in much the same way, though the roots are very tedious to scrape; in the past I suspect they grew better skirrets than seem possible now. Mine are always like a mass of thin thongy roots instead of the salsify-like ones described in old books. The following are a personal selection of the more interesting old vegetables I have tried.

Beetroot – 'Bulls Blood': blood-red leaves that look pretty grown with flowers; gives a useful crop of beetroot; 'Barbabietola di Chioggia': an Italian beetroot whose inside is striped pink and white; it looks very decorative sliced raw, but the flavour is not particularly special.
Broad bean – 'Green Windsor': the best-tasting broad beans I have grown; the tender, bright green beans freeze well too.
Broccoli, early purple sprouting: like small purple cauliflower florets at the tips of stems; for picking early spring when fresh vegetables are scarce.
Brussels sprout – 'Noisette': tiny, slightly crunchy, nutty sprouts that are both delicious sliced raw and cooked whole.

Sow the seed of the cauliflower 'Purple Cape' in mid- to late spring and the heads will be ready for cutting the following late winter to early spring. This cauliflower turns green when cooked, leaving the purple colour behind in the water.

Cabbage – 'Early Jersey Wakefield': large pointed hearts up to 0.9–1.4kg (2–3lbs) in weight; Collards: a type of cabbage rather than a specific variety, grown for spring greens rather than hearts.

Carrot – 'Oxheart': very old, early, broad stump rooted carrot.

Cauliflower – 'Purple Cape': a purple-headed cauliflower with a lovely, buttery taste; it takes almost a year to mature.

French bean, climbing – 'Marvel of Venice': large, flat yellow pods, cooked whole when small, or grown on and shelled like peas; 'Pea Bean': short, curvy pods with beans of a stunning flavour and jigsaw-puzzle shaped markings in cream and maroon; shell and use like peas, or dry and store for winter.

French bean, dwarf – 'Mont d'Or': yellow-podded bean; stringless pods; superb buttery flavour.

Kale – 'Cottagers': pretty, curly leaves with mauve stalks; the young shoots are eaten in spring when there is little else available fresh from the garden.

Lettuce – 'Rouge d'Hiver': a delicious-tasting French red cos lettuce for winter and spring cropping; it is slow to bolt; Cos lettuce – 'Balloon', 'Vaux's Self Folding', 'Winter Density' and 'Lobjoits': all these are solid, tasty lettuces, which, once the leaves start to stand upright, need tying round with raffia; this keeps the leaves close together over the heart, encouraging the leaves to 'blanch' which improves the flavour and holds the shape of the lettuce; Miniature cos – 'Little Gem': one of the best-tasting lettuces still available; it needs no tying.

Orache: a very ancient pottage herb, used for flavouring the thick oatmeal soup that was once the standard fare of early cottagers; red orache is much prettier; it is cooked and eaten like spinach but turns an odd colour when cooked; grows up to 2m (6ft) high and is also valued as an ornamental plant among flowers, and for flower arranging.

Potato – 'Pink Fir Apple': long, narrow tubers which are very firm and well-flavoured; good in salads.

Runner bean – 'Painted Lady': pretty bi-coloured flowers (orange and very pale pink), but the beans are disappointing in flavour; 'Mrs Cannell's Black Runner': black seeds passed round among enthusiasts, and not commercially available; peachy coloured flowers, and very tender, tasty beans.

ABOVE *The runner bean 'Painted Lady' (1855) is a much loved old cultivar with unusual white and orange flowers.*

LEFT *The cos lettuce 'Balloon' (1885) should be tied round with raffia as soon as it starts to grow upright after the rosette stage, to encourage the formation of a tight heart. It is well worth the effort as the lettuce tastes wonderful and has a very crisp texture.*

Collector's plants

SUGGESTED CULTIVARS OF PINKS

'Caesar's Mantle': the 'bloody pink'; single, deep carmine scented flowers; 25cm (10in).

'Charles Musgrave': single, large white, heavily fringed flowers with distinct green centre; scented; 23cm (9in).

'Fenbow's Nutmeg Clove': dark red, strongly scented flowers, to 45cm (1½ ft).

'Grandad's Favourite': semi-double laced pink; white petals with a 'laced' chestnut-maroon pattern; 20cm (8in).

'Queen of Sheba': unusual single, red, scented flowers feathered with cream; weak stems; 15cm (6in).

'Red Emperor': double crimson-pink fringed flowers that open early and continue well; scented; 25cm (10in).

'Unique': single maroon-red scented flowers strongly patterned with white stripes and streaks; 15cm (6in).

'Waithman's Beauty': the 'clock-faced' pink; scented red flowers with pale pink markings; 15cm (6in).

Elsewhere in this book we have seen how very popular plants like herbs for example (see pages 30–1) for which a large range of species or cultivars exist, can be put together to make a theme area. But with small collections of more specialized plants you need to take a slightly different approach to integrate them into the garden. You might, for example, use a collection of hardy geraniums or campanulas for ground cover throughout a particular part of the garden, making the collection the continuous link that pulls together a general planting scheme.

Small plants, and those that are fussy about their soil and/or situation, are best given their own beds. Primroses, hardy ferns and hellebores, for instance, all need permanent moisture and lots of organic matter in the soil, and dappled shade overhead (see also show auriculas on page 28). Once you have made a bed for a particular plant, you can then choose other, similar-sized and non-invasive plants to grow with them and set them off. Look especially for companions that flower when the star plants do not, to avoid detracting from them, as well as extending the season of interest of the bed. Plants that need particularly well-drained conditions can be grown in a small raised bed, perhaps built from old, loose-laid bricks, or dry stone walling – preferably the material that is used for old walls locally. Other small plants, or those needing extra special attention, could be grown in pots or tubs by the back door or by a seat (see page 64). This is ideal for lime-hating plants such as blueberries, if you have a chalky soil.

If you collect plants with a short flowering season, you cannot expect a specialist bed to be a blaze of colour over most of the summer. To extend the season of interest, you can intermingle the collection with other compatible plants, but it is inevitable, when working in a small space with plants that have short flowering seasons, that a bed will only look its best for a short time every year. Most collectors avoid this problem by arranging the garden so that the centre of interest moves round throughout the year, via a number of different seasonal features, rather than having only borders containing a mixture of

plants for all seasons. A series of short, seasonal cameos makes a small garden more interesting. Instead of looking the same from early summer to autumn, it takes on a completely altered appearance at the onset of each mini-season.

Growing pinks

Old pinks (*Dianthus*) suffer from the problem of a short flowering season, but nevertheless have great appeal for the cottage garden collector. Old cultivars of pinks need an open, sunny situation and well-drained soil with little organic matter added. Choose similar-sized planting companions that enjoy the same conditions but will not overwhelm the pinks, such as slow-growing rock plants. I like my pinks to be stars of their own bed, so I deliberately choose plants that complement them but play a supporting role, rather than trying to steal the limelight. I also plant quite close together (about 30–45cm/1–1½ft between plants) so that the ground is completely covered by the time any pinks need replacing.

Propagation

Old pinks need propagating every two to three years as they are short-lived plants. Take softwood cuttings 8cm (3in) long in early mid-summer after the plants have finished flowering. Nip out the growing tip of the shoots between thumb and forefinger and carefully peel away the leaves from the lower half of the cutting. Dip the cut ends into rooting hormone, then ease into slits made in a pot of sandy seed compost composed of equal parts of seed compost and horticultural or silver sand. Firm them in, taking care not to push them as you would pelargoniums as the stems are too soft and bendy. Cuttings take about four weeks to root in a cold frame or cold greenhouse in light shade and need to be kept just moist. Pot individually and grow on until late summer/early autumn when they can be planted out into beds. If soil or other growing conditions are not ideal, plants can be held over under cover for the winter, for planting the following spring. In my experience most rock plants grown with pinks also benefit from a fresh start at about the same time.

Growing roses

Old-fashioned roses are very different from modern cultivars and may present particular problems. Many, such as *Rosa* 'William Lobb', have tall, rather weak stems that need supporting to prevent the plants flopping about all over the place. One of the most cottagey ways of doing this is to make a tripod of rustic poles, and place it over the plant so the new growth comes up through the middle. Some of the small-growing cultivars, such as 'Camaieux' and 'Robert le Diable', have very weak stems that terminate in heavy flowers which bend down to the ground, making them impossible to see properly. I support these roses by tying their stems to short garden canes, but a large herbaceous plant support frame should work equally well.

Virtually all rose plants sold by nurseries, including old-fashioned roses, consist of two plants grafted together – the roots of a rootstock variety, grown for

its strong root system, and the stems of the named variety. Some modern roses would scarcely survive without grafting as their own roots are very weak. Old roses, however, would originally have been grown on their own roots. They are, in fact, easily propagated from softwood cuttings, approximately 15cm (6in) long with their soft tips removed, in mid-summer and treated like pelargoniums, though they take longer to root (see page 96).

Old roses should not be pruned like Hybrid Teas but more like normal shrubs. I summer-prune old-fashioned roses when dead-heading, by cutting back the flowered shoots to the nearest new shoot or decent-looking growth bud. At the same time I cut out any weak growth, and generally tidy up the plant's shape. In late autumn I trim back the long shoots that have grown during the summer by about half, to prevent wind-rock. Hard pruning is certainly to be avoided, as it encourages a massive growth of suckers from grafted plants. Since suckers are a nuisance from time to time anyway, I generally prefer to grow my old roses on their own roots.

ABOVE Rosa *'Jacques Cartier'*, a bourbon rose introduced in 1868, produces a main flush of flowers in early summer, followed by occasional blooms throughout the rest of the season.

LEFT Dianthus *'Waithman's Beauty'* is called the 'clock-faced' pink because the two pale pink dashes on each petal are reminiscent of the intervals on a clock face.

A rose garden

Old-fashioned roses suffer from the same problem as old-fashioned pinks – a short flowering season. The centrepiece of this garden, shown in early mid-summer, is a climbing *Rosa* 'Cécile Brunner' grown as a large bush – this will continue flowering all summer. The other roses, with the exception of 'Jacques Cartier' which does produce a few flowers at a time after the main flush is over, bloom only in early mid-summer. Enthusiasts underplant their old-fashioned rose collections thickly with a patchwork of cottage garden plants, designed to be at their best when the roses are not.

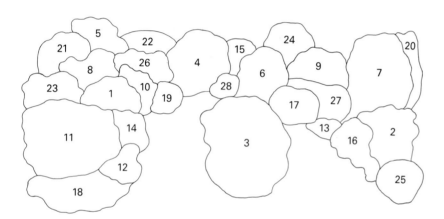

Roses

1 'Camaieux': small plant, up to 90cm (3ft); scented, double, pale pink flowers with reddish-mauve stripes.

2 'Cardinal de Richelieu': compact plant, growing up to 120cm (4ft); scented, double, dusky purple flowers.

3 'Cécile Brunner, Climbing': makes a large, mound-shaped plant 3–3.7m (10–12ft) tall when grown as a bush tree instead of trained up a wall; pale pink flowers all summer.

4 'Charles de Mills': medium-sized plant, up to 120cm (4ft); scented, double, reddish purple flowers.

5 'Fantin-Latour': large vigorous plant, up to 1.5m (5ft); rather flat, pale pink flowers.

6 *R. gallica* 'Versicolor', syn. *R. mundi*: small plant, growing up to 90cm (3ft); large, semi-double, red flowers splashed and striped with pink and white.

7 'Great Maiden's Blush': large plant, up to 1.5m (5ft); glaucous foliage; scented, double, pale pink flowers.

8 'Jacques Cartier': compact small plant, up to 90cm (3ft); scented, flattish, pale pink flowers; recurrent flowering.

9 'Robert le Diable': small plant, up to 90cm (3ft), with mauve-red flowers highlighted

with lilac and shaded with purple.

10 'Tour de Malakoff' ('Black Jack'): large plant, up to 1.8m (6ft); purple shaded magenta flowers fading to lilac-grey.

11 'William Lobb' ('Old Velvet Moss'): moss rose; large vigorous plant, up to 1.8m (6ft); flowers change colour as they age from pink-red buds through to dove grey.

Accompanying plants

12 *Astrantia major rosea*: rose-pink flowers in summer and autumn; herbaceous perennial growing to 45cm (1½ft).

13 *Astrantia major* 'Sunningdale Variegated':

off-white flowers tinged pink and green in summer and autumn; lime and cream variegated foliage; 45cm (1½ft) high herbaceous perennial.

14 *Campanula persicifolia* 'Double Blue': 75cm (2½ft) spikes of mid-blue flowers in summer; herbaceous perennial.

15 Chimney bellflower (*Campanula pyramidalis*): 1.5m (5ft) spikes of blue or white flowers in summer; biennial.

16 *Geranium endressii* 'Wargrave Pink': low mounds of foliage covered with single, silvery pink flowers mid- to late summer; herbaceous perennial.

17 *Geranium pratense* 'Plenum Violaceum': double, purple-mauve flowers mid-summer; grows to a height of 75cm (2½ft); herbaceous perennial.

18 *Geranium procurrens*: spreading, creeping species; single mauve flowers from mid-summer to autumn; herbaceous perennial.

19 Gold feverfew (*Tanacetum parthenium* 'Aureum'): low, self-seeding evergreen; lime-green foliage and clusters of yellow-centred white daisies most of the summer.

20 Hollyhock (*Alcea rosea*): 1.8–2.2m (6–7ft) stems with double or single pink, rose or maroon flowers all summer; technically a perennial; often grown as an annual because it is likely to suffer from hollyhock rust.

21 *Lilium auratum*: yellow-striped white flowers with red-brown spots in mid-summer; stems grow to 1.8m (6ft); prefers acid soil.

22 *Lilium* 'Green Magic': ghostly green-tinged white flowers on 120cm (4ft) stems in mid-summer.

23 *Lilium martagon* var. *album*: lots of white turk's cap flowers on 120cm (4ft) stems in early mid-summer; lime-tolerant.

24 *Lilium regale*: huge, white, funnel-shaped, scented flowers on 90–150cm (3–5ft) stems in mid-summer; lime-tolerant.

25 *Nepeta racemosa*, syn. *N. mussinii*: low bushy plant with mauve-purple flowers all summer; grey foliage; hardy perennial.

26 *Salvia × superba*: 90cm (3ft) violet-purple spikes of flowers mid- to late summer; herbaceous perennial.

27 *Sisyrinchium striatum*: iris-like leaves with 60cm (2ft) stems lined with small cream flowers in summer; herbaceous perennial.

28 *Stachys byzantina*, syn. *S. lanata*: grey 'lamb's ears' leaves; felty spikes studded with pink flowers in summer; semi-evergreen shrub.

Bellis perennis
'Prolifera'

The hen and chickens daisy is a quaint, old-fashioned plant that was once grown in pots on the window sills of unheated cottages. It is a close relative of the daisy you find in lawns, but each flower, the 'hen', is surrounded by masses of tiny, identical flowers dangling from thread-like stems, the 'chickens'. Although not very easy to keep, the hen and chickens daisy is so charming that it is well worth the effort. It should be grown in fertile soil, which should not be allowed to dry out because of the very shallow roots. Occasional light feeding and regular treatment against greenfly is also required. If successful, it also needs dividing regularly. Plants are not that easy to find today but they are occasionally on sale at nurseries specializing in old-fashioned flowers.

Cultivating choice plants

Part of the fun of cottage gardening lies in searching out choice plants. Enthusiasts enjoy driving out into the country at weekends to visit remote nurseries in order to hunt for plant 'treasures'. Some specialist nurseries also send out mail-order lists, but their choicest plants are usually available in quantities too small to list, so they are only available to personal callers. Plant fairs, at which large numbers of small, specialist nurseries are gathered together, are well worth a visit. These are a relatively new way of plant hunting but a day at a plant fair can save you weeks of travelling to each nursery in turn. Another good way of finding choice plants is by joining specialist plant societies (see page 32).

Propagation

Once you have managed to obtain scarce or choice plants it is vital to propagate from them, as it may prove very difficult to replace your original plant should you lose it. Scarce plants are often rare because they are either hard to propagate, or hard to grow – sometimes both. A lot of choice cottage garden plants are also very short-lived, like old pinks and named perennial wallflowers, and must be propagated regularly to replace elderly plants before they die. Once you have propagated something special, it is a good idea to give a few 'spares' to fellow enthusiasts, besides keeping some for yourself. This way, you know where to obtain fresh propagating material if your stock dies out. The other advantage of giving away choice plants is that you will probably be given other plants in return. This is the way most plant enthusiasts work, and build up a close circle of friends into the bargain.

Softwood cuttings

Softwood cuttings are the easiest way of propagating most cottage garden plants that cannot conveniently be divided. You can use quite short pieces of stem, down to 2–5cm (1–2in) lengths with plants that have only short stems. Some groups of plants have specific propagation requirements, while others are very easy-going and root readily at any time of year. I

apply the following general rule. For plants that flower in spring or early summer, take soft cuttings in late summer to early autumn. For plants that flower after mid-summer, take cuttings in late spring. There is, however, a lot to be said for the theory that the best time of year to take a cutting is when one is offered to you – on the grounds that the offer may not be repeated at the right time!

Softwood cuttings of most cottage garden plants are prepared as you would pelargoniums. Remove the leaves from the lower half of the cutting and trim off the base of the stem neatly under a leaf joint with a sharp knife (see right). Dip the cutting into rooting powder and push into sandy compost of equal quantities of seed compost and silver sand. For small quantities, it is most convenient to use a 9cm (3½in) pot with five cuttings around the edge, but for larger quantities use a seed tray. Water in, and stand the pot or tray inside a propagating case, or under a cold frame or plastic cover of some sort to retain humidity. Check frequently and remove mouldy leaves or dead cuttings, and water to keep the compost from drying out.

Softwood cuttings usually take between four and six weeks to root. Test by tugging gently or carefully digging up a cutting with a small dibber. When well-rooted, the young plants should be potted individually in 9cm (3½in) pots of potting compost and grown on until they are big enough to plant out in the garden safely – about the size of the smallest plants you would buy at a nursery.

Irishman's cuttings

Irishman's cuttings are taken from plants whose stems creep along the ground and tend to produce a few small wispy roots above the ground while the stems are still attached to the parent plant – a common occurrence with many cottage garden plants. These partially rooted shoots are torn from around the edges of the plant and then potted as they are into 9cm (3½in) pots of seed or multi-purpose compost. They do, however, need treating with more care than normal rooted cuttings as, of course, they are barely rooted. Treat them as cuttings for the first few weeks as regards level of care, then as young plants after their first potting.

Tuberous plants

For plants with tubers, such as dahlias and *Cosmos atrosanguineus*, propagate at the start of the growing season. The basic method of propagation is from softwood cuttings taken from the first shoots to appear when the tubers start into growth. This is vital as the rooted cutting must form a small tuber of its own to be able to survive the winter. As dahlias are not planted outdoors until mid-spring, no shoots will appear above ground before late spring or thereabouts. It is necessary then to start dahlias into growth artificially by removing the tubers from winter storage and spraying them with water on the bench in a heated greenhouse (or frost-free porch or similar) in early spring. With cosmos, however, the tubers are much smaller and in mild areas plants prefer to be left in the soil over winter. Otherwise, they are best grown in large pots and plunged into the ground, and then lifted, still in their pots, and stood in a cold frame for the winter. This way you need to wait until the first shoots appear above ground naturally since the tubers are never exposed. This will probably not occur until early summer.

Division

When dividing perennial plants, I again apply a general rule; for those plants that flower early in the year, divide in autumn, and for those that flower late in the year, along with more delicate plants, divide

Chocolate-scented cosmos (Cosmos atrosanguineus) is one of the great success stories of plant conservation. Originally from Mexico, the plant declined in cultivation as it set only sterile seed and so had to be propagated from cuttings. After a successful campaign publicizing its plight, it is now widely available.

in spring. The whole clump of the plant should be dug up with a fork and then pulled into pieces with your hands (see below). If the roots are too matted and cannot be divided by hand, push two garden forks, back to back, through the middle of the clump and use them to prise the roots apart. Discard any old material from the centre of the clump and, after preparing the soil (see page 36), replant only healthy young pieces from round the edges.

Softwood cuttings and hand division

A cutting 15cm (6in) long has been taken from an *Argyranthemum* 'Jamaica Primrose'. This is then trimmed to 10cm (4in), just below a leaf junction, and the leaflets from the lower half of the cutting removed so that the stem is clean for insertion into the compost (see 1, right). Clump-forming perennials are best propagated by division. Some can be divided simply by pulling sections apart by hand (see 2, right). The divided sections should be replanted to the same depth as before.

1 *Trim the stem with a sharp knife and remove the lower leaves.*

2 *Divide a clump-forming perennial by pulling it apart into sections by hand.*

Cottage garden favourites

The original cottagers relied on their gardens to provide a wide range of household necessities from rheumatic remedies to good luck charms, as well as the edible varieties of fruit, vegetables and herbs. The 'nouveau' cottagers of Victorian and Edwardian times, however, were far more interested in creating instant nostalgia and growing plants purely for their appearance and scent. Whatever your interests, a few cottage garden curios dotted around the garden can be relied on to add 'olde worlde' atmosphere – and to get your visitors talking (see pages 100–1).

Traditional plants

Rosa rubiginosa, syn. *R. eglanteria*, the sweet briar or eglantine, is one of the most traditional cottage garden plants. It has small pink flowers, but its chief attraction is the delightful scent of apples given off by the foliage when it is damp or after rain. The perennial double wallflowers, *Cheiranthus cheiri*

*Sweet rocket (*Hesperis matronalis*) is a biennial plant with single pink or white flowers which add a lingering scent of spice to mid-summer evenings. Once established, a colony will self-seed.*

'Bloody Warrior' and 'Harpur Crewe', are probably the only survivors of a bigger range available around the turn of the century, when evidently black and green double wallflowers were available. Double wallflowers do not set seed and are short-lived, so must be propagated from softwood cuttings every year or two in summer (see page 96).

Mignonette (*Reseda odorata*) and sweet rocket (*Hesperis matronalis*) are two old cottage favourites rarely seen today though seed is available through the catalogues of the big seed firms. The flowers of mignonette are unspectacular greeny yellow spikes, with a very sweet scent. A hardy annual, sow in spring for summer flowers or autumn to use as a spring-flowering pot plant for a cold room, as earlier cottagers once did. Sweet rocket has white or mauve single flowers; doubles were once popular but are mostly lost now – the only remaining kind has scented lilac flowers. It must be propagated vegetatively, that is, from cuttings.

Lilium candidum is one of the oldest cultivated plants, and has been grown in cottage gardens for many centuries. Myrtle (*Myrtus*) is an evergreen shrub grown for its flowers, fruits and aromatic foliage. According to custom, myrtle bushes were 'passed down' on marriage. Sprigs were included in a bride's bouquet and if these rooted and grew, the new wife would plant them by her front door and it was believed she would enjoy a happy marriage. If her bridesmaid took pieces of myrtle to root and they failed to strike, she would remain an old maid.

Several other cottage plants had medicinal and witchcraft uses. Lungwort (*Pulmonaria*) is one of the old medicinal herbs believed, under the doctrine of signatures, to cure lung problems since its spotted leaves were thought to resemble tubercular lungs. Self-heal (*Prunella vulgaris*) was grown by the side of carpenter's shops in old villages, as a quick first-aid remedy for cuts. Vervain (*Verbena officinalis*) was used in ancient druid rites and later in black magic then medicine, while henbane (*Hyoscyamus niger*), a poisonous plant, was once employed by witches to induce convulsions in their victims, and by horse dealers to quieten highly strung livestock. Betony (*Stachys officinalis*, syn. *Betonica officinalis*) was used to protect people from the effects of witchcraft. Rue (*Ruta graveolens*) has various medical uses; nosegays of it were once used in courtrooms to protect judges from the noxious germs and vapours brought up from the gaols by prisoners on trial.

Plants for household use

Insect repellents Fleabane (*Pulicaria dysenterica*): coarse wild plant with slightly felted leaves and yellow daisy-like flowers in summer, 75cm (2½ft) tall; burnt to repel fleas; herbaceous perennial.

Pennyroyal (*Mentha pulegium*): small creeping mint-like plant with lavender flowers from mid- to late summer; minty/insecticidal-smelling leaves; also used to repel fleas; herbaceous perennial.

Southernwood (*Artemisia abrotanum*): soft aromatic foliage; used to repel moths from wardrobes; herbaceous perennial.

Tansy (*Tanacetum vulgare*): 90cm (3ft) tall plants with 'prince-of-wales' feather-like leaves; yellow button flowers in late summer; leaves were rubbed over meat to deter flies; herbaceous perennial.

Laundry Soapwort (*Saponaria officinalis*): low-growing plant with small leaves and lots of tiny pink flowers in summer; leaves produce a soapy substance when frothed in warm water; once used for washing delicate clothes; perennial.

Perfuming linen Lavender (*Lavandula angustifolia*): dried lavender flowers were put into muslin bags and slipped into drawers or cupboards to scent clothes; semi-evergreen subshrub.

Orris root (*Iris* 'Florentina'): white-flowered iris, whose dried roots when ground into powder smell of violets; used to perfume linen stored in chests, and to fix the scent of pot-pourri; herbaceous perennial.

Roseroot (*Rhodiola rosea*): small, succulent plant with greenish-pink flowers in early summer, whose dried roots are rose-scented and used for perfuming linen; herbaceous perennial.

Dyes Dyer's chamomile (*Anthemis tinctoria*): low bushy plant smothered with yellow daisy flowers in summer; yields a yellow dye; herbaceous perennial.

Dyer's greenweed (*Genista tinctoria*): small shrub with bright green stems and yellow pea-flowers; tops of shoots yield a yellow dye.

Dyer's weld (*Reseda luteola*): tall biennial with greenish-yellow flowers, yielding a yellow dye.

Woad (*Isatis tinctoria*): very tall, untidy branching plant with glaucous stems and leaves, and yellow daisy flowers; the leaves when fermented yield a dark purplish-blue dye, reputedly used by Ancient Britons; biennial.

Flavourings for drinks Alecost (*Balsamita major* var. *tanacetoides*): also called 'mace'; balsam-scented plant 60–90cm (2–3ft) high with large, toothed, spicy-tasting leaves used to flavour mulled ale; herbaceous perennial.

Clove pink (*Dianthus caryophyllus*): strong, sweet, clove-scented flowers that were used as a flavouring for mulled wine; perennial.

The flowers of pennyroyal (Mentha pulegium) are individually small but are grouped together to attract insects. In moist soil, the plant can be rather invasive.

An old-fashioned border

The old-fashioned curiosities in this border, illustrated here in early mid-summer, all have a history attached to them and make fascinating conversation pieces (see pages 98–9).

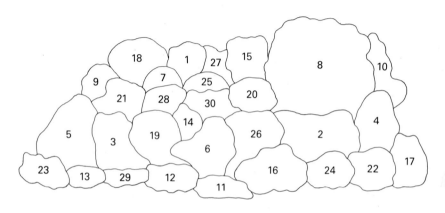

1 *Anthemis tinctoria*: large, golden, daisy flowers from early to late summer; aromatic, feathery foliage, grows 60–90cm (2–3ft) high; herbaceous perennial.

2 Bergamot (*Monarda didyma*): red flowers arising from a central boss all summer; 60cm (2ft) high; herbaceous perennial.

3 Betony (*Stachys officinalis*, syn. *Betonica officinalis*): makes a 30cm (1ft) high spreading mat of foliage covered in summer with pink flowers; herbaceous perennial.

4 *Cheiranthus cheiri* 'Bloody Warrior': double red flowers with yellow edging in early summer: 45cm (1½ft) short-lived perennial.

5 *Cheiranthus cheiri* 'Harpur Crewe': double yellow flowers in early summer; 45cm (1½ft) short-lived perennial.

6 Clove pink (*Dianthus caryophyllus*): evergreen foliage and purple-pink, scented flowers in early to mid-summer; grows to 13cm (5in); perennial.

7 *Cosmos atrosanguineus*: rather sparse, low-growing foliage; semi-double, maroon-chocolate, scented flowers all summer; grows to about 60cm (2ft); perennial.

8 Eglantine (*Rosa rubiginosa*, syn. *R. eglanteria*): shrub growing to 2.5–3m (8–10ft) in height and width; pale pink flowers in mid-summer and red hips in autumn.

9 Gilded rosemary (*Rosmarinus officinalis aureus*): slightly untidy evergreen bushy shrub unevenly splashed with gold; now rather rare.

10 Globe artichoke: silvery green foliage and large, mauve thistle heads mid-summer; grows 1.8–2.5m (6–8ft); herbaceous perennial.

11 Gold creeping jenny (*Lysimachia nummularia* 'Aurea'): straight stems and pairs of gold leaves; herbaceous perennial.

12 Heartsease (*Viola tricolor*): tiny wild pansies with pale yellow and lilac faces, flowering early to mid-summer; short-lived

perennial that behaves more like an annual.

13 Hen and chickens daisy (*Bellis perennis* 'Prolifera'): same shape and size as the lawn daisy but has lots of 'chicks' hanging from the central 'hen' flower; early to mid-summer flowering; 8–10cm (3–4in); perennial.

14 Henbane (*Hyoscyamus niger*): upright stems to 30cm (1ft) with odd-shaped leaves; creamy flowers from mid-summer; poisonous annual.

15 *Lilium candidum*: white, scented, trumpet-shaped flowers in early mid-summer; 90–120cm (3–4ft) high.

16 Lungwort (*Pulmonaria officinalis*): large, oval, spotted leaves with clusters of pink and blue flowers on 30cm (1ft) stems in late spring; herbaceous perennial.

17 Mignonette (*Reseda odorata*): 30cm (1ft) high hardy annual; oval leaves; fragrant green-yellow flowers in summer and early autumn.

18 Myrtle (*Myrtus communis*): small, evergreen, bushy shrub with single cream flowers in mid- to late summer.

19 *Nepeta racemosa*, syn. *N. mussinii*: 30cm (1ft) high catmint covered in mauvish flowers from early to late summer; hardy perennial.

20 Old english lavender (*Lavandula × intermedia* 'Old English'): semi-evergreen shrublet with silvery leaves and purple flowers in summer; the flowers reach 90cm (3ft) but the foliage is much lower.

21 Orris root (*Iris* 'Florentina'): white flowers in early summer; for the rest of the season the foliage contrasts nicely with other flowers.

22 Pot marigold (*Calendula officinalis*): hardy annual to 45cm (1½ft) with bright orange flowers in summer; self-seeding.

23 Rose plantain (*Plantago major* 'Rosularis'): short-lived perennial; green flower spikes grow to 15cm (6in); self-seeding.

24 Roseroot (*Rhodiola rosea*, syn. *Sedum rosea*): succulent herbaceous perennial growing to 30cm (1ft); yellow-green flowers in summer.

25 Rue (*Ruta graveolens*): low, evergreen, bushy plant with striking, densely packed, blue-grey leaves; rather unattractive yellow flowers in summer.

26 *Silene dioica* 'Rubra Plena', syn. *Melandrium rubrum*: loose, double, red-pink flowers on 60cm (2ft) stems in early summer; foliage forms tight-spreading ground cover 5–8cm (2–3in) high; herbaceous perennial.

27 Skirret (*Sium sisarum*): resembles cow parsley, 90–120cm (3–4ft) tall; flowers late mid-summer; herbaceous perennial.

28 Sweet rocket (*Hesperis matronalis*): biennial with 45cm (1½ft) spikes of lavender, white or purple flowers from spring.

29 Variegated wild strawberry (*Fragaria vesca* 'Variegata'): evergreen perennial, ground cover plant; bright cream and green leaves; small white flowers early to mid-summer.

30 Vervain (*Verbena officinalis*): 60cm (2ft) spikes of pink flowers in mid- to late summer; herbaceous perennial.

THROUGH
THE SEASONS

Each season brings something new to the garden – something different to look at, and something different to do. But whereas in conventional gardens plants tend to be chosen for their long flowering periods, and seasonal changes are therefore that much slower, the cottage gardening year consists of a series of bursts of brief flowering – albeit overlapping – each creating a mini-season with new highlights of its own.

In spring, bulbs provide most of the colour in the cottage garden. Low-growing species are useful for naturalizing in grass under trees, and taller kinds for grouping together informally. The tulips in the foreground here are 'White Triumphator', one of the lily-flowered cultivars which have narrow-waisted, single flowers, and 'Dancing Show', one of the viridiflora cultivars which have a pronounced green stripe down the middle of each petal.

Spring

Spring is one of the two main seasons in the cottage garden, the other being mid-summer. Fruit-tree blossom and bulbs provide the main highlights, but there are also plenty of smaller, choicer treasures to enjoy, such as gold-laced polyanthus, double primroses and double celandines. Areas of moist, dappled shade will shelter clumps of the common primrose, the drum-stick primrose (*Primula denticulata*), wood anemones, bergenias, violets, *Euphorbia amygdaloides robbiae*, snake's head fritillary (*Fritillaria meleagris*), hellebores and hardy *Cyclamen coum*. In the hedges, hazel catkins are starting to appear. In borders, early pulmonarias, *Symphytum* 'Rubrum', *Alyssum saxatile*, doronicums, wallflowers, aubrieta, *Euphorbia characias wulfenii* and *Iberis sempervirens* all look pretty teamed with bulbs such as snowflakes (*Leucojum vernum*), daffodils and the first waterlily tulips (*Tulipa kaufmanniana*). Of the old cottage garden shrubs, flowering currant (*Ribes sanguineum*), bridal wreath (*Spiraea × arguta*), and japonica are the seasonal stars. And in the vegetable garden, kale and 'Purple Cape' cauliflower will be ready to pick, along with the last of the late sprouts and leeks.

Flowers

Get flower borders off to a good start by digging up and dividing any summer- and autumn-flowering herbaceous plants that need rejuvenating (see page 97). Weed the beds, then spread a 5cm (2in) thick mulch of any well-rotted organic matter over any exposed soil, tucking it carefully around emerging shoots, and placing handfuls into the crowns of plants such as hardy cranesbills which tend to 'grow themselves out of the ground' (see page 39). Plant up any new beds (see pages 41 and 56), then mulch between the plants as above. Sow hardy annuals in trays and protect under a

Naturalized spring flowers for light shade.

cold frame or in a cold glasshouse or porch. Alternatively, when the soil has warmed up a little, sow them directly into borders that are free of weed seeds, or in rows in the vegetable garden for transplanting. Plant dahlias by placing tubers stem-side up in holes 15cm (6in) deep towards the end of the season so that new shoots are not damaged by late frosts. Plant lily bulbs (see page 122).

Fruit and vegetables

Mulch around tree and soft fruit; clear the remains of winter vegetables, such as leeks, brussels sprouts, sprouting broccoli and kale, once they have finished and dig the ground over. Spread blood, fish and bone or other general purpose fertilizer at the manufacturer's recommended rate, and rake the ground level; when the soil has warmed up in mid- to late spring, sow leeks, summer and autumn cabbage, kale, brussels sprouts, lettuce and most other vegetables except those that are not frost-hardy. Plant the sprouted tubers of potatoes.

Propagation

Take softwood cuttings of dahlias shortly before the tubers are planted out, and 'Irishman's cuttings' of many clump-forming plants, such as hardy cranesbills and london pride (see page 96). Indoors, take any extra cuttings you might need from half-hardy perennials such as pelargoniums, and pot up over-wintered cuttings struck last year in 9cm (3½in) pots depending on their root size, to grow on until after the last frosts when they can be planted outside. Sow half-hardy annuals on a warm window sill as early as possible.

Early summer

By now, the early spring flowers are slowly being replaced by a new crop: tulips, canterbury bells, dicentra, brunnera, the early hardy cranesbills, aquilegia, honesty, lady's mantle, forget-me-nots, wallflowers, peonies and oriental poppies, very quickly followed by old-fashioned pinks, which often last only a few weeks. Spring blossom now gives way to lilac, broom (which country folk still think unlucky), hawthorn and *Kerria japonica*, together with late flowering fruit trees such as medlars and elders. If you have cottage garden treasures such as show auriculas, move the pots to a good situation in light shade where you will enjoy them most (see page 28). In the vegetable garden, lettuce, baby carrots and other early crops will be ready to pick.

Bulbs

Snip off flowerheads of early spring bulbs when they are over; do not tie daffodil foliage into knots or mow the foliage of bulbs naturalized in grass: wait for at least six weeks after the flowers have died, otherwise you may spoil the following year's flowering. Sprinkle superphosphate around, or water with tomato feed to help build up the bulbs for next year.

Flowers

Dead-head early flowers as they go over. Once the risk of frost is past in your area, plant out zinnias, nicotianas and other half-hardy annuals, and tender perennials such as pelargoniums. Pot-grown flowers can be planted at any time, even when in flower, as long as you do not disturb the roots when knocking them out of their pots. Fork a little organic matter into the soil first, and water the plants afterwards. Keep all new plants well watered in dry spells. Plant up any containers using potting compost. When you have moved them to their final positions, check them daily throughout the summer to see if they need watering, as containers dry out very quickly, especially in warm or breezy weather. Bear in mind that peat-based composts retain more water than other kinds.

Fruit and vegetables

Tuck straw or special fibre mats between strawberries to prevent the fruit from touching the damp soil, which can cause it to rot. Drape nets over soft fruit and strawberries to deter birds. Allow soft fruit to ripen completely on the plants, and pick every two days. Cut asparagus spears, but remember to leave some on the plants at the end of the cutting season (early mid-summer) to develop into the ferny foliage that the plants need in order to regenerate themselves (see page 70).

Make regular sowings of lettuce seeds and those of other fast-maturing salad leaves like rocket (*Eruca versicaria sativa*), not to be confused with sweet rocket (*Hesperis matronalis*), to ensure a continuous supply; cut them regularly, too, to avoid plants running to seed and wasting. Gather herbs and leaf salads little and often, whenever you need them. Pick herbs for drying or freezing before any flower buds appear. Sow or plant tender crops such as french beans and courgettes after the last risk of frost in your area (see page 70).

A summer planting of herbaceous flowers.

Mid-summer

Roses are the stars of high summer, with old-fashioned cultivars putting on a spectacular show lasting only a few weeks, and climbers and ramblers providing a more enduring display on arches and walls. Clematis are at their peak, too, as are the great mass of herbaceous flowers: the garden should now be a colourful tumble of hollyhocks, delphiniums, campanulas, lilies, phlox, evening primrose, bergamot, catmint, penstemon and other traditional flowers. This is also the time for cottage economy enthusiasts to gather flowers for drying, petals to make pot-pourri, and berries for summer puddings, wine, jam making or freezing.

Flowers

Plant autumn-flowering bulbs, such as colchicums and autumn crocus, as soon as they become available (see page 41). Continue dead-heading flowers as they go over in order to encourage plants to keep producing new flowering stems. Summer-prune old-fashioned roses by cutting back flowered shoots to a new growth bud, which will be approximately 15–20cm (6–8in) below the dead flowers. Remove very weak growth entirely, and tidy up the shape of the plant at the same time. Repeat-flowering roses, such as bourbons and repeat-flowering climbers, should be treated less severely: simply 'dead-head' by cutting back to a growth bud up to 5–8cm (2–3in) back, or to a strong new shoot.

Every three years, dig up and divide bearded irises about six weeks after they have finished flowering. Discard old rhizomes from the centre of the clump, and replant strong pieces from round the edge. Choose a sunny spot, or they will not flower; prepare the soil well with a good general fertilizer such as blood, fish and bone, and well-rotted compost, and plant the rhizomes shallowly, with their tops exposed above the surface of the soil. Cut down the foliage of oriental poppies if it is taking up too much room, otherwise simply remove the dead flower stems in order to avoid leaving a large, unsightly gap in the border. Support the stems of dahlias as the heavy flowers develop by hammering four strong, wooden stakes into the ground around the plants and tying thick, strong string between and across the stakes, to form a grid through which the stems grow.

Fruit and vegetables

Prune berry and cane fruit as soon as you have finished picking them (see pages 86–7). Gather broad beans and other early vegetables, clear the ground, and take the opportunity to fork in extra organic matter, if available, and sprinkle general fertilizer over the soil at the manufacturer's recommended rate to replenish nutrients. Continue sowing lettuce and start sowing early cultivars of peas. These will both be ready for harvesting by the autumn.

Propagation

Old-fashioned pinks live for only two to three years, so take softwood cuttings regularly to replace old plants (see page 93). Plants will be ready to put out in autumn. Many easy shrubs, roses and herbaceous plants can also be rooted from softwood cuttings taken early in mid-summer. Take short cuttings from the non-flowering tips of side-shoots and pot them as you would old-fashioned pinks. To encourage rooting, place the pots inside large, loose plastic bags, with a couple of small perforations in them, for a week or two. This will help to retain humidity around the leaves.

Late summer

Once again the garden takes on an entirely new look, as the flowers of mid-summer give way to those of the later season. Japanese anemones, sunflowers, cottage chrysanthemums, *Sedum spectabile*, dahlias and michaelmas daisies (*Aster novi-belgii*) are all seasonal favourites, and it is also worth hunting for some more unusual plants, such as schizostylis, *Aster amellus* and *A. ericoides* cultivars, russian sage (*Perovskia atriplicifolia*) and toad lilies (*Tricyrtis formosana* Stolonifera Group), to add interest and detail. Some summer flowers will keep going well into late summer if regularly dead-headed: penstemons are especially useful in this respect. Late-flowering clematis, such as the *Clematis viticella* hybrids, now come into their own, and some early-flowering cultivars, such as 'Bees' Jubilee', 'Barbara Jackman', and 'Nelly Moser' give a short late flush around this time; double-flowered clematis often produce a brief flush of single flowers in late summer too. Hybrid Tea roses can be guaranteed to keep flowering right up to the first frost, though the ripening fruits of species roses, crab apples, rowans, medlars, and apples and pears are much more cottagey looking in late summer gardens.

Medlar fruit and autumn foliage tints.

Flowers

Continue dead-heading flowers as they go over; towards the end of summer, however, you can start to tidy up borders by cutting back complete stems of early herbaceous plants that are starting to die back. Leave the seedheads of teasels and sunflowers for the birds to enjoy. Plant spring-flowering bulbs such as daffodils. Daffodils are among the first of the spring-flowering bulbs to start rooting and should be planted as soon as the bulbs become available in the shops (see page 41). Tulips root later on, so need not be planted until autumn.

Fruit and vegetables

Eat early apples, such as 'Beauty of Bath' and 'Irish Peach', straight from the tree as they do not keep. Leave other apples to continue ripening on the tree. Gather the pods of french beans that have been left on the plants to dry for winter use in soups and casseroles. Shell the beans and put them in a cool oven to finish drying. They should then be stored in airtight jars. Plant spring cabbage. Early leeks and brussels sprouts will be ready to eat towards the end of this season. Cut down asparagus foliage when it turns yellow.

Propagation

Take soft tip cuttings of half-hardy perennial plants such as pelargoniums, fuchsias and verbenas, root them into pots or trays of seed compost, and keep them on a sunny window sill indoors or in a frost-free porch or greenhouse for the winter. This way you can avoid having to dig up and pot the old plants and finding room for them indoors for the winter. Left outside, they would be killed by the cold.

Autumn

Harvest is the theme of the cottage garden in autumn, as fruit and vegetables are gathered for winter storage. Although autumn colour is not a traditional feature of cottage gardens, it is not difficult to arrange a few autumnal 'cameos' round the garden, based on hips, berries, nuts, seedheads and late flowers. Crab apples, rowans and hawthorn berries will remain on the trees for a while yet; for late flowers choose *Hydrangea paniculata* and *H. arborescens*, *Clematis* 'Lady Betty Balfour' (bluish) and 'Madame Edouard Andre' (wine-red); *Clematis tangutica* and *Physalis alkegengi franchetii* bear attractive seedheads, and autumn foliage colour is provided by medlar, serviceberry (*Amelanchier*) and *Hydrangea quercifolia*. Autumn-flowering bulbs such as colchicums and autumn crocus add a splash of brighter colour, and some late summer flowers go on flowering well into the autumn, notably hardy fuchsias, penstemons and schizostylis. In early autumn, you could tuck in plenty of clumps of the earliest snowdrops (*Galanthus*) in spots where you cannot miss their delicate flowers – a sure sign that spring is on its way. Plant tulip bulbs for flowering in spring.

Beneficial insects

Do not be too zealous about clearing borders round the edge of the garden, as debris provides valuable over-wintering sites for beneficial insects such as centipedes, ground beetles and spiders. In spring these will be quick to colonize your garden, eating a wide range of pests without your needing to resort to chemicals. Next year, encourage more beneficial insects to the garden by sowing or planting a mixture of wild flowers in and around the garden: they look quite at home in cottage gardens, and their nectar attracts predatory insects such as hoverflies.

Storing vegetables

On clay soils, dig up root crops such as parsnips before the winter wet begins. The most practical way to store root crops, given the less than perfect storage conditions normally available nowadays, is to dry them off and store in open mesh sacks in a frost-free shed, or suspended in a 'hammock' from the roof (which allows you to pick them over and remove rotten ones with ease). Do not wash the soil off as they keep better dirty. Do not attempt to keep them too long as they will start to shrivel after a few weeks. Root crops in light, well-drained soil can be left until required for use. Leave leeks, brussels sprouts, kale and cabbage in the ground as well, until needed.

Storing fruit

Apples and pears are ripe for picking when they lift easily from the tree when cupped in the palm of your hand; pick any that remain by mid-autumn at the latest. To keep well, fruit needs a cool, dark place with humidity and a steady temperature, ideally 4–7°C (40–45°F). In the absence of a traditional fruit-store room, a well-insulated shed, attic or very cool spare bedroom could be used. For the sake of convenience, put cultivars that keep the longest to

Hoar frost on the hips of Rosa *'Scarlet Fire'.*

the back of the storage area. Place those that will need using quickly towards the front. Stand the fruit in shallow trays, not quite touching each other. Slatted trays are the traditional choice because they can be stacked without impeding the circulation of air through the layers of fruit; if you have to use solid trays, store them only one layer deep. Check stored fruit regularly; remove any that are shrivelled for cooking and throw rotting ones away.

Winter

Cottage gardens have never been all year round gardens, but by including low edging of box, pieces of topiary, and cottagey evergreen features such as ropes of ivy (made by twisting the stems of trailing types round as they grow) strung along the edge of a path, you can outline the garden in such a way that it still looks pretty even without flowers to decorate it. Making garden 'compartments' helps here too – a formal herb garden (see pages 72–3), for

instance, can be based on an all-year-round framework of evergreen species such as rosemaries and thymes for winter interest. Make the most of such winter flowers as there are: *Iris unguicularis* will flower on and off throughout the winter in a well-drained position against a sunny wall, and wintersweet (*Chimonanthus praecox*), *Prunus × subhirtella ascendans* 'Autumnalis', *Viburnum farreri* and christmas rose (*Helleborus niger*) all bloom in late winter, although a sheltered site is essential to prevent the winter flowers being damaged by bad weather. Group winter flowers together for the greatest impact.

Planning

For most people the winter break, when the garden is dormant, is the best time of the year for planning. Now is the opportunity to reorganize on paper parts of the garden that did not look quite right last year, or to plan any new features that you want to put in. This is also the season for the new crop of seed catalogues, so you can choose which flowers and vegetables to order. Specialist societies send out their seed lists during this time, too, and if you want to learn something new, gardening societies hold most of their meetings in the winter, on the grounds that members are too busy gardening during the rest of the year. Some clubs arrange discounts for members buying seeds or other garden sundries, or come to arrangements with local garden centres, so membership can bring other rewards as well.

Pruning

Prune bush and standard trees in the winter when they are dormant; any time between leaf fall in autumn and bud burst in spring. There is no need to prune standard trees at all if you do not want to, but well-pruned trees will yield fewer but bigger fruit, which will also be better coloured, as light and air will be able to penetrate the thinned branches more easily.

KEY PLANTS

Traditional cottage garden plants will always remain the basis of any cottage garden scheme, no matter how many newer, more fashionable plants you include. Many are like old friends, and it is always a pleasure to see them again after a seasonal break. Others, though unspectacular in their own right, fulfil the valuable function of providing continuity in the garden, helping to create the peaceful ambience that is essential to the cottage garden's sense of calm.

The nodding, cup-shaped flowers of the lenten rose (Helleborus orientalis) appear in early spring. Available in a wide variety of colours, including dark purple, green and white, this perennial thrives in well-drained soil in shady corners of the garden. Named cultivars are highly prized by collectors.

Old-fashioned plants make up only a part of today's cottage garden. However, as they are the plants that do most to establish the 'flavour' of the garden, I have concentrated on them here. I have also included my personal favourites, on the grounds that cottage gardens are self-indulgent gardens intended to provide homes for all your favourite plants. So, when planting your cottage garden, do feel free to indulge your passion, whether it be for alpines, wild flowers, unusual trees or shrubs, or modern herbaceous plants.

Some of the plants I have included in this chapter are species, such as *Cosmos atrosanguineus* and gardener's garters (*Phalaris arundinacea* var. *picta*), largely because they are 'one-offs'. Wherever possible, though, I have given more general groups, such as cottage chrysanthemums (*Dendranthema rubellum*), as this gives more scope to write about a few extra plants. But some entries cover much 'looser' plant groups, such as hardy annuals. This, again, allows me to discuss a greater number of plants, and since the plants in these groups are all raised and used in much the same way, I felt they benefited from a slightly different treatment.

A word of explanation is needed about the brief summaries following each plant description. This information is based largely on my own experience, and does not always coincide exactly with that provided by nursery catalogues and reference books.

Anemone japonica

Herbaceous perennials

Adiantum pedatum see under Ferns

Alchemilla mollis
(Lady's mantle)

Neatly pleated grey-green leaves and masses of frothy lime-green flowers in early to mid-summer make lady's mantle a useful filler all round the garden. It is also a good background plant, providing a visual link between more flamboyant flowers. Moreover, it grows almost anywhere, and self-seeds happily in the right conditions – the perfect cottage garden plant. It is also valued for its versatility in flower arrangements.
Size H: 30cm/1ft; S: 45cm/1½ft. **Aspect** Sun or shade. **Hardiness** Very hardy. **Soil** Any. **Planting partners** Goes with almost anything, especially with *Euphorbia amygdaloides robbiae* and ferns in shade, and with campanula and herbs or roses in sun.

Anemone japonica
syn. *Anemone × hybrida*
(Japanese anemone)

After the main summer display is over, japanese anemones bring the garden back to life with their elegant late-summer and autumn flowers. Named cultivars offer a choice of pink or white flowers, single or semi-double. All are slow to establish, but then tend to spread and so need curtailing every year or two.
Size H: 69–90cm/2–3ft; S: 90cm/3ft. **Aspect** Sun or part-shade. **Hardiness** Very hardy. **Soil** Any reasonably moisture-retentive. **Planting partners** *Aster novae-angliae*, *Liriope muscari*.

Aquilegia vulgaris
(Columbine, granny's bonnets)

Flowering in late spring and early summer, aquilegias overlap with the last of the bulbs and the first of the roses. Though technically perennials, they behave more like biennials in my garden. They are also enthusiastic self-seeders. Whatever colours you start with – and aquilegias come in all shades of yellow, pink, mauve, purple, blue and red, including bicolours – you will soon have a glorious mixture, as they cross-pollinate randomly.
Size H: 75cm/2½ft; S: 30cm/1ft. **Aspect** Sun or part-shade. **Hardiness** Very hardy. **Soil** Any not too dry. **Planting partners** *Brunnera*, bluebells, *Lunaria annua variegata*, *Silene dioica* 'Rubra Plena'.

Asplenium scolopendrium
see under Ferns

Astrantia major
(Masterwort, hattie's pincushion)

Astrantia is good for cutting but I prefer to leave it in the garden where it makes a good filler between more spectacular plants, and is most effective growing under roses. It self-seeds nicely. The shaggy flowers are not particularly striking but the pink *Astrantia major rubra* and the variegated leaved 'Sunningdale Variegated' deserve a spot where they will be noticed.
Size H: 30cm/1ft; S: 45cm/1½ft. **Aspect** Sun. **Hardiness** Very hardy. **Soil** Any; tolerates dry conditions. **Planting partners** *Salvia purpurea*, roses, lavender.

Athyrium niponicum pictum
see under Ferns

Bachelor's buttons
see *Ranunculus acris*

Bellflower see *Campanula*

Campanula

(Bellflower)

Campanulas are available in a wide variety of species and sizes. The taller forms are especially useful, with spikes of blue-mauve or white flowers emerging from a sea of cottage garden plants or echoing other tall spiky shapes. Rampion (*Campanula rapunculoides*) is grown for its 75cm (2½ft) spikes of blue summer flowers, while the clustered bellflower (*C. glomerata*) at 45cm (1½ft) can spread alarmingly. My favourite is *C. persicifolia* (45cm/1½ft), especially the double powder-blue forms. Campanulas need heavy feeding and moving occasionally to a new site with well-prepared soil; propagate by division. (See also *Campanula* under Annuals and biennials.)
Size H and S: Varies with species. **Aspect** Light shade or in a sunny border tucked between taller plants. **Hardiness** Hardy. **Soil** Rich, fertile, well-drained but moist, with lots of organic matter. **Planting partners** *Nicotiana alata, Nigella*.

Cheiranthus cheiri see under Annuals and biennials

Chocolate-scented cosmos
see *Cosmos atrosanguineus*

Christmas rose see *Helleborus*

Columbine see *Aquilegia vulgaris*

Convallaria majalis

(Lily-of-the-valley)

Lily-of-the-valley, with its wonderful scent, flowers just after most of the spring bulbs are over. Buy pot-grown plants or beg roots from a friend, and transplant in autumn or shortly after flowering in a moist, shady spot or under shrubs. Lily-of-the-valley is slow and difficult to establish; be sure to keep plants well mulched so the roots do not dry out.
Size H: 1–1.5m/3½–5ft; S: 60cm/2ft. **Aspect** Shady. **Hardiness** Hardy. **Soil** Moist, well-drained but containing plenty of organic matter. **Planting partners** Shrubs.

Cosmos atrosanguineus

(Chocolate-scented cosmos)

A fascinating flower which almost vanished from cultivation. Chocolate-scented cosmos looks like a very small dahlia, with single maroon-black flowers smelling strongly of plain chocolate. The tuber is not very hardy, and in my garden of clay soil succeeds best grown in pots sunk into the ground for the growing season, and moved to a frost-free greenhouse for the winter. In a well-drained spot, it survives mild winters outdoors when planted 8cm (3in) deep and given a thick mulch. Flowering in late summer, the plant is also late to appear above ground in spring.
Size H: 60cm/2ft; S: 30cm/1ft.

Aquilegia vulgaris

Herbaceous perennials, the mainstay of the summer cottage garden, cover a wide range of shapes, sizes, colours, textures and plant habits. It is the contrast between these that 'makes' a traditional cottage border.

Aspect Sun. **Hardiness** Not reliably hardy. **Soil** Well-drained. **Planting partners** *Diascia, Sedum spectabile, Salvia officinalis* 'Tricolor'.

Cottage chrysanthemum see
Dendranthema rubellum

Cottage peony
see *Paeonia officinalis*

Cranesbill see *Geranium*

Euphorbia characias wulfenii

Dendranthema rubellum
(Cottage chrysanthemum)

These very old-fashioned flowers have yet to regain the popularity of other traditional cottage garden flowers, but they are well worth growing for their very late pompon flowers, which often go on into mid- to late autumn. Unlike exhibition chrysanthemums, these are left in the ground permanently and are divided in early spring every few years. Good cultivars include 'Bronze Elegance' (amber-bronze), 'Emperor of China' (deep rose-pink) and 'Anastasia' (mauve-pink).

Size H: 60–75cm/2–2½ft; S: 45–60cm/ 1½–2ft. **Aspect** Sun. **Hardiness** Very hardy. **Soil** Any reasonably well-drained. **Planting partners** Each other.

Dianthus
(Pink)

Modern pinks such as *Dianthus* 'Doris' flower throughout the summer, but the old-fashioned cultivars generally have a stronger scent and more character, even though they only flower for a few weeks in mid-summer. (In a hot summer, some kinds will have another flush of flowers in early autumn or thereabouts). Interesting old cultivars include 'Charles Musgrave' ('Old Green Eye'), semi-double white with a green centre; 'William Brownhill', double white with brownish maroon lacing; 'Waithman's Beauty' (the 'clock-faced' pink), single red with pale pink dashes on each petal giving a flower that looks like a clock-face; and 'Fenbow's Nutmeg Clove' which I am sure is actually a border carnation as it is a much stronger grower than the others, with double red flowers. Pinks are short-lived and need propagating every two to three years; take cuttings soon after flowering; pot when rooted and plant out in autumn.

Size H and S: 30cm/1ft. **Aspect** Sun. **Hardiness** Hardy. **Soil** Chalky, with little or no organic matter; well-drained. **Planting partners** *Artemisia schmidtiana* 'Nana', *Gypsophila paniculata* 'Rosy Veil' ('Rosenschleier'), *Hebe* 'Carl Teschner'.

Digitalis
(Foxglove)

Foxgloves are useful flowers for a shady corner or in moist soil under trees. As well as the wild foxglove, *Digitalis purpurea*, try more unusual species such as *D. lutea* with its spikes of small yellow funnel-shaped flowers, *D. lanata* which has strange pouch-like flowers in pearl with bronze dots and a pronounced lip, and the rather shorter *D. purpurea heywoodii* (75cm/2½ft) which has silvery leaves and pale creamy pink flowers.

Size H: 1.5m/5ft; S: 30cm/1ft. **Aspect** Shade or dappled shade. **Hardiness** Hardy. **Soil** Moist. **Planting partners** Grow in front of a shady wall planted with *Clematis* 'Comtesse de Bouchaud', *C.* 'Hagley Hybrid', *C.* 'Nelly Moser', and shade-tolerant climbing roses such as *Rosa* 'Bleu Magenta', *R.* 'Russell's Cottage Rambler' (syn. *R.* 'Russelliana') and *R.* 'Souvenir du Docteur Jamain'.

Euphorbia
(Spurge)

Though not really authentic cottage garden plants, spurges are newly fashionable plants which have found good homes there. *Euphorbia amygdaloides robbiae*, with low rosettes of evergreen leaves and greenish flowers in spring, is useful for ground cover in shady spots or sun. For partial shade, *E. amygdaloides purpurea* and *E. dulcis* 'Chameleon' both have prettily coloured foliage. The family also includes some tall, strikingly architectural plants for sun and reasonably well-drained soil; especially good are *E. characias wulfenii*, *E. mellifera* and *E. sikkimensis*.

Size H and S: Varies according to species. **Aspect** Sun or partial shade, according to species. **Hardiness** Hardy. **Soil** Shade-tolerant kinds like some moisture; sun-lovers need well-drained to dry conditions. **Planting partners** In shade, *Alchemilla mollis*, *Helleborus*; in sun, *Kniphofia*.

Ferns, hardy

Invaluable for cool shady corners, hardy ferns have also become very collectible, so an interesting selection is now available. The evergreen hart's tongue fern (*Asplenium scolopendrium*) is one of my favourites; several cultivars have crested foliage. The hardy maidenhair fern (*Adiantum pedatum*) has foliage like the pot plant. The japanese painted fern (*Athyrium niponicum pictum*) is most spectacular, with red stems and silver variegated fronds, but not very hardy – mine stays in its pot and comes into the greenhouse in winter. Plant hardy ferns in soil enriched with lots of organic matter for moisture retention, and see that they never dry out.

Size H and S: 45cm/1½ft. **Aspect** Shade to dappled shade. **Hardiness** Hardy except japanese painted fern. **Soil** Cool, moisture-retentive. **Planting partners** *Astilbe*, *Primula denticulata*, *Polygonatum × hybridum*, *Viola labradorica*.

Foxglove see *Digitalis*

Fuchsia

Nowadays there are hardy fuchsias available with large showy flowers that look very much like pot plant fuchsias, but for authentic cottage garden types choose *Fuchsia magellenica* and *F.* 'Riccartonii' which have narrow-petalled flowers in mauve and red. Both can also be grown, in authentic cottage garden style, as low, flowering hedges. Cut hardy fuchsias down to ground level in winter and cover the site with ashes, bracken or organic matter to protect the roots from freezing. It is important to feed plants generously during the growing season, mulch to keep the soil moist, and water in very dry spells.

Size H and S: 90cm/3ft. **Aspect** Partshade. **Hardiness** Hardy. **Soil** Rich, reasonably well-drained. **Planting partners** Bourbon roses, *Lavatera*.

Gardener's garters see *Phalaris arundinacea* var. *picta*

Geranium
(Cranesbill)

Cranesbills are another very collectible group of plants, making good ground cover beneath roses and taller cottage garden plants. In shade, grow *Geranium macrorrhizum*, which has pink or mauvish flowers in early summer, or *G. phaeum* (dusky cranesbill), with purple-black flowers also in early summer; cultivars are available with lilac or white flowers. Other species prefer to have more sun: *G. pratense* (meadow cranesbill) is best for ground cover in a wildish area as it spreads quickly and it is happy growing in grass.

Choicer species for growing in a border include *G. psilostemon* (mound-shaped plants bearing shocking magenta flowers with black eyes in early summer), *G. endressii* 'Wargrave Pink' (also mound-shaped, with sil-

very pink flowers in mid- to late summer), *G. pratense* 'Plenum Violaceum' (very pretty double purple-mauve flowers in summer) and *G. procurrens* (a sprawling species with single mauve flowers from midsummer through to autumn).

Size H: 30–60cm/1–2ft; S: 30–90cm/1–3ft according to species. **Aspect** Most prefer sun at least half the day. **Hardiness** Very hardy. **Soil** Good, reasonably well-drained. **Planting partners** Roses, *Verbascum*.

Geranium pratense 'Mrs Kendall Clarke'

Granny's bonnets see *Aquilegia vulgaris*

Hattie's pincushion see *Astrantia major*

Lychnis coronaria with *Lavandula* 'Hidcote'

Helleborus
(Christmas rose, lenten rose)

The christmas rose (*Helleborus niger*) has white single flowers which normally appear in mid-winter; in early spring the lenten rose (*H. orientalis*) bears its spotted flowers in shades of pink, mauve, green, white and smoky purple – named cultivars are much sought after. The green-flowered stinking hellebore (*H. foetidus*) blooms in early spring and does not stink unless interfered with. Hellebores are useful plants for shady corners and under trees, though they also grow in sun if the soil is not too dry. Most have attractive evergreen leaves which provide a good background for summer flowers. Leave the flower-heads to self-seed, as they often produce interesting seedlings. These transplant well, but leave mature plants undisturbed if possible; move them in winter if you must.
Size H: 30–60cm/1–2ft; S: 45cm/ 1½ft. **Aspect** Shade or part-shade for

preference. **Hardiness** Hardy. **Soil** Fertile, moisture-retentive but free-draining. **Planting partners** *Cyclamen coum*, early daffodils (*Narcissus*), snow-drops (*Galanthus*), violets (*Viola*).

Houseleek see *Sempervivum*

Japanese anemone see *Anemone japonica*

Lady's mantle see *Alchemilla mollis*

Lavandula
(Lavender)

Herb specialists list a good range; old english lavender (*Lavandula × intermedia* 'Old English') has silvery leaves and purple flowers, while 'Hidcote Pink' has pink flowers. *L. lanata* (woolly lavender) is low-growing with intense silvery leaves and purple flowers; *L. stoechas* (french lavender) is rather tender, and *L. stoechas pedunculata* has a pair of large wing-like petals sprouting from the top of the flower-head. All are good as dried flowers and in pot-pourri; dried florets and leaves of french lavender can also be used as a culinary herb. Lavenders are perennials, semi-evergreen, and dislike hard pruning – clip them lightly with shears after flowering to reshape them. They propagate easily from cuttings. A row makes a good low hedge or edging to a formal herb garden.
Size H: 30–60cm/1–2ft; S: 30cm/1ft. **Aspect** Sun. **Hardiness** Hardy; *L. stoechas* is slightly tender. **Soil** Well-drained; will tolerate dry conditions. **Planting partners** Herbs, roses.

Lenten rose see *Helleborus*

Lily-of-the-valley see *Convallaria majalis*

Linaria purpurea

Although it looks so cottagey, *Linaria* is not an especially traditional flower. A well-behaved, self-seeding perennial, it bears tall, narrow, elegant spikes of purple toadflax flowers, which look delightful nosing up through clumps of heavier blooms or contrasting foliage. Let it wander through a herbaceous border for a light airy touch. The species has light purple flowers, and an equally pretty pink form called 'Canon Went' is also available. Both flower in mid- to late summer, and often into the autumn. I have never needed to buy plants or seed – mine have all arrived from the village on the wind.
Size H: 90cm/3ft; S: 15cm/6in. **Aspect** Reasonably sunny. **Hardiness** Very hardy. **Soil** Any. **Planting partners** Artichoke, pink gypsophilas such as *Gypsophila paniculata* 'Flamingo' and 'Rosy Veil'.

Lychnis coronaria
(Rose campion)

This traditional summer-flowering cottage garden plant is often overlooked by modern gardeners. The species has shrieking magenta flowers which stand out well in a border, and are ideal for making a pool of colour amongst foliage. Pure white and pink-and-white forms are also available, and

though not half so striking, they go very well with the silver foliage. All self-seed fairly freely and have pleasant silvery-felted stems and leaves.
Size H: 60–90cm/2–3ft; S: 30–45cm/1–1½ft. **Aspect** Reasonably sunny. **Hardiness** Very hardy. **Soil** Any. **Planting partners** Tall artemisias or grasses, silver foliage.

Masterwort see *Astrantia major*

Paeonia officinalis
(Cottage peony)

Most modern peonies are *Paeonia lactiflora* cultivars which flower in midsummer, but the true cottage peonies, which flower a month earlier, are *P. officinalis* cultivars and are now quite hard to find; 'Rosea Superba Plena' (double pink) and 'Rubra Plena' (double crimson) are among the most widely available. Both *P. officinalis* and *P. lactiflora* types need to be planted so that the buds are 2.5cm (1in) below the surface of the soil. Contrary to popular belief, it is possible to move peonies at most times of year with success, though you usually then find the plant growing in both its original site and the new site. This is because they propagate themselves from bits of root left behind at the original site, which then grow up to make new plants. The biggest problem with peonies is that they leave such a big gap in the border when they are over. This can be avoided, however, by cutting the stems down three weeks after they have flowered and planting annuals around their crowns.

Size H and S: 75cm/2½ft. **Aspect** Sun. **Hardiness** Hardy. **Soil** Deep, rich, well-drained but moisture-retentive with lots of organic matter. **Planting partners** None; plant so that later flowering plants provide a background of foliage.

Penstemon campanulatus
(Penstemon)

Penstemons bear spires of large trumpet flowers in a good range of colours over a long season (from mid-summer into early autumn), tolerate drought conditions and mix well with other plants in the garden. Good cultivars include 'Garnet' (burgundy), 'Apple Blossom' (pale pink), 'Mother of Pearl' (as the name suggests), 'Alice Hindley' (mauve-blue flower with a white throat), and the flower arranger's favourite, 'Sour Grapes' (a blend of amethyst, sea green and blue).
Size H: 60–75cm/2–2½ft; S: 30cm/1ft. **Aspect** Sun. **Hardiness** Not very hardy; over-winter rooted cuttings as a precaution. **Soil** Rich with plenty of organic matter, but fairly well-drained. **Planting partners** *Argyranthemum foeniculaceum* 'Chelsea Girl', *Osteospermum*.

Phalaris arundinacea
var. *picta*
(Gardener's garters, ribbon grass)

A useful grass with ribbon-like green-and-white striped leaves, gardener's garters grows anywhere, in sun or shade, and even in very poor dry soil. Best grown with other rampant spreaders and self-seeders, it looks

especially good among brightly coloured ones; if left loose in a bed of treasures, however, it will quickly swamp them. It makes good weed-resistant ground cover under trees and shrubs, or for filling odd bits of ground where you do not want much work. It dies down in winter.
Size H: 60cm/2ft; S: 75cm/2½ft. **Aspect** Sun or shade. **Hardiness** Very hardy. **Soil** Any; tolerates both wet and dry conditions. **Planting partners** *Borago officinalis*, *Lychnis chalcedonica*, *Papaver orientale*.

Pink see *Dianthus*

Linaria purpurea and *L. purpurea* 'Canon Went'

Phlox paniculata
(Phlox)

Good fillers for a border in mid- to late summer, after the old roses are over, phlox also make a good background for the more striking flower spikes and frothy textures of the middle of the border. Available in a huge range of colours, from coral reds, salmon, lilac, and all shades of pink to pure white, they are easily propagated from cuttings in spring or summer.
Size H: 60–90cm/2–3ft; S: 45cm/1½ft. **Aspect** Sun, or part-shade between other plants. **Hardiness** Hardy. **Soil** Any fairly fertile and moisture-retentive. **Planting partners** *Delphinium*, repeat-flowering roses, *Thalictrum delavayi* cultivars.

Ranunculus acris
'Flore Pleno'
(Bachelor's buttons)

A number of cottage garden plants seem to have acquired the name bachelor's buttons over the years; this one, a double form of the wild meadow buttercup with tightly packed balls of yellow petals, appears to have been discovered as a wild sport in the fifteenth or sixteenth century. It does not spread as rampantly as the wild buttercup, and flowers in early and mid-summer.
Size H: 75cm/2½ft; S: 45cm/1½ft. **Aspect** Sun. **Hardiness** Very hardy. **Soil** Moist. **Planting partners** *Corylus avellana* 'Contorta', *Iris versicolor*.

Ribbon grass see *Phalaris arundinacea* var. *picta*

Rose campion see *Lychnis coronaria*

Sempervivum
(Houseleek)

These hardy, succulent-leaved, rosette-shaped plants which bear curious spires of flowers in mid-summer will grow quite happily in the most inhospitable, hot, dry, sunny situations. They used to be grown on the roof of old cottages or outbuildings to deter lightning (or so it was said); you can still grow them this way by throwing up handfuls of soil followed by a few unrooted rosettes. Nowadays they are more often grown in sinks or pots by a doorway, in gritty alpine-type soil. They also look very attractive edging a gravel path, or growing in gaps between paving.

Many varieties of houseleek are available from nurseries specializing in alpine plants. The cobwebbed houseleek (*Sempervivum arachnoideum*) has silver hairs connecting the tips of the leaves; others have smooth red, bright green, chocolate or patterned bodies, or exceptionally large rosettes.
Size H: 8cm/3in (30cm/1ft when in flower); S: 23–30cm/9in–1ft. **Aspect** Sun. **Hardiness** Hardy. **Soil** Well-drained, fairly poor and gritty. **Planting partners** *Sedum*.

Silene dioica
'Rubra Plena'
syn. *Melandrium rubrum*

The double form of the wild red campion is now a scarce old cottage garden plant that deserves to be better known. The plant makes a loose carpet of leaves, above which 30–45cm (1–1½ft) stems carry rather open pink semi-double flowers in late spring and early summer. It looks best grown among plenty of other flowers to hide its slightly untidy nature.
Size 30–45cm/12–18in. **Aspect** Part-shade to light shade. **Hardiness** Hardy. **Soil** Any reasonably moisture-retentive. **Planting partners** *Geranium phaeum*, honesty (*Lunaria annua*).

Spurge see *Euphorbia*

Viola
(Violet)

All sorts of violets are old cottage favourites. *Viola labradorica* (with soft mauve flowers and purple leaves) seeds itself in shady flower beds, sunny gravel paths, and even lawns. *Viola odorata* (the wild sweet violet) comes in several cultivated forms, many of which are Victorian forms, and in various shades, including pink. Some violets, such as the cultivar 'Czar', have large flowers, which are very good for cutting, and most are strongly scented. The rare and exquisitely scented parma violets should be grown in cold frames in winter.
Size H and S: 8–15cm/3–6in. **Aspect** Light shade. **Hardiness** Mostly hardy, though parma violets need protection in winter. **Soil** Moisture-retentive but reasonably well-drained. **Planting partners** Primroses (*Primula vulgaris*).

Wallflower see *Cheiranthus cheiri* under Annuals and biennials

Annuals and biennials

Alcea rosea
(Hollyhock)

Hollyhocks are probably the first plants most people think of when cottage gardens are mentioned. Although perennials, they are usually grown as annuals in order to try and combat hollyhock rust. If you buy plants or grow them from seed from a catalogue, you will have the choice of some very fancy varieties, with black or double flowers for example. Sow the seed in spring or early summer for flowering the following year. However, if you let hollyhocks self-seed, they will revert in time to the semi-wild cottage garden sort, with pink or mauve flowers. These can be left to continue self-seeding, which they do very successfully into gravel paths and cracks in concrete or paving.

Size H: 1.8–2.1m/6–7ft; S: 60cm/2ft. **Aspect** Some direct sun preferred. **Hardiness** Hardy. **Soil** Any. **Planting partners** Grow in clumps on their own close to the house.

Annuals, half-hardy

Although they are all too often associated with parks department bedding schemes, some half-hardy annuals are nevertheless cottage garden essentials. They include old-fashioned favourites like *Nicotiana* (see page 119), everlasting flowers such as statice (*Limonium*) and helichrysum, climbers such as morning glory (*Ipomoea purpurea*), and asters and zinnias for cutting. Half-hardy annuals can be grown from seed in a heated greenhouse or on a warm sunny window sill indoors. Otherwise, buy them from a garden centre, and plant them out after the last expected frost in your area. Good soil and a sunny aspect are essential. Plant in clumps for best effect.

Annuals, hardy

Colourful, inexpensive hardy annuals are useful for a quick display when starting a new garden, or for filling odd gaps that can appear during the season in even the best-planned garden. They can be sown where you want them to flower, provided the soil is free from weed seeds; otherwise they can be sown in rows in the vegetable garden for transplanting, or in pots, pricked out and planted when large enough to compete. Some will self-seed. The best types for a cottagey effect include nasturtiums (*Tropaeolum majus*), cornflowers (*Centaurea cyanus*), shirley poppies (*Papaver rhoeas*), english marigolds (*Calendula*), sunflowers (*Helianthus*), forget-me-nots (*Myosotis alpestris*), godetia, larkspur (*Delphinium consolida*) and night-scented stock (*Matthiola bicornis*). All need reasonably good soil and a sunny situation, and they are best planted in small tight groups for an authentic cottage garden look.

Campanula medium
(Canterbury bell)

Canterbury bells are traditional cottage garden plants, flowering in late spring to early summer with huge pink, white or blue bells on 75cm (2½ft) stems. Different cultivars or seed mixtures offer a choice between bell-shaped flowers or the intriguing

Campanula medium

Old-fashioned annuals and biennials are in danger of being neglected in modern gardens. However, groups of annuals and biennials look good filling gaps in borders where, with briefer flowering perennials, they provide continuity of colour.

cup and saucer flowers (which have a 'disc' of petals behind the bell to form the saucer). (See also *Campanula* under Herbaceous perennials.)

Size H: 75cm/2½ft; S: 20cm/8in. **Aspect** Very light shade – between other tall plants for instance. **Hardiness** Benefits from some shelter in winter. **Soil** Any good, fertile, reasonably well-drained. **Planting partners** *Lunaria annua*.

*Lunaria annua
variegata*

Campanula pyramidalis
(Chimney bellflower)

This biennial campanula is also well worth growing: though less traditional than the canterbury bell, it still looks cottagey, and in addition it is extremely useful. The 1.2–1.5m (4–5ft) spikes of flower, borne in mid-summer, look good grown amongst tall plants towards the back of the border, and are superb for cutting. (See *Campanula* under Herbaceous perennials.)
Size H: 1.2–1.5m/4–5ft; S: 30cm/1ft. **Aspect** Very light shade (between other tall flowers). **Hardiness** Not as hardy as *C. medium*; needs shelter. **Soil** Any good, fertile, reasonably well-drained. **Planting partners** *Malva*, repeat-flowering roses.

Canterbury bell
see *Campanula medium*

Cheiranthus cheiri
(Wallflower)

Any tall bedding wallflowers look cottagey, but I prefer an old mixture called *Cheiranthus cheiri* 'Persian Carpet'. Bedding wallflowers are technically perennials but treated as biennials, raised from seed every summer to plant the same autumn for flowering the following spring. Perennial wallflowers are sought-after old flowers now; 'Bloody Warrior' (double red with yellow frills round the edge of the petals) and 'Harpur Crewe' (tight double yellow buttons) are the only doubles left. There are also some fascinating singles, in shades from two-tone mauve to metallic bronze. Propagate from cuttings every year as the plants are short-lived.
Size H: 60cm/2ft; S: 20–30cm/8in–1ft. **Aspect** Sun. **Hardiness** Hardy. **Soil** Any reasonable soil, fairly well-drained. **Planting partners** Parrot tulips.

Chimney bellflower
see *Campanula pyramidalis*

Evening primrose
see *Oenothera biennis*

Hollyhock see *Alcea rosea*

Honesty see *Lunaria annua*

Lathyrus odoratus
(Sweet pea)

Useful climbers for growing informally up trellises, arches or tripods of canes, sweet peas are hardy annuals, more easily grown from an early spring sowing rather than an autumn one, as is the practice of exhibitors. Feed frequently with liquid or soluble plant feed at the highest strength recommended by the manufacturer. Deadhead regularly or they will quickly stop flowering. Frequent cutting helps too. Grow *Lathyrus odoratus* 'Painted Lady' if you can get seed: some seed firms supply old-fashioned sweet pea mixtures. Even more cottagey is the everlasting pea (*L. latifolius*): grown on a sunny wall it will bear its small magenta flowers all summer.
Size H: 1.5m/5ft; S: 30cm/1ft. **Aspect** Sunny for at least half the day. **Hardiness** Hardy. **Soil** Rich, moisture-retentive with lots of organic matter. **Planting partners** *Delphinium*, roses.

Lunaria annua
(Honesty)

A biennial plant with purplish flowers in late spring followed by large clusters of the familiar white, flat, elliptical seedheads in summer, honesty usually self-seeds readily once established. A white-flowered form, *Lunaria annua alba*, is also available, as is one with variegated leaves, *L. annua variegata*. Scarcer is 'Stella' which has both white flowers and variegated leaves. It is beautiful though rather frail. Also very cottagey is *L. rediviva*, a short-lived perennial honesty with pale lilac flowers.
Size H: 75cm/2½ft; S: 30cm/1ft. **Aspect** Part-shade. **Hardiness** Hardy. **Soil** Any. **Planting partners** Late daffodils, *Geranium phaeum*.

Nicotiana
(Tobacco plant)

The real old cottage garden flowering tobacco, *Nicotiana alata* (syn. *N. affinis*), has tall stems of white flowers that are heavily scented in the evening, but which hang limply during the day if grown in sun, so if possible choose a shady position for planting. *N. langsdorfii* has apple-green, almost bell-like, flowers and taller stems (90–120cm/3–4ft instead of 75cm/2½ft). *N. sylvestris* grows to 1.5m (5ft) tall, and has huge oval leaves and great bunches of long, trumpet-like white flowers erupting from the top of the stems. Nicotianas are half-hardy annuals. New plants should be grown every year from seed.

Size H: 1–1.5m/3½–5ft; S: 60cm/2ft. **Aspect** Sun or shade. **Hardiness** Not hardy. **Soil** Rich, moist. **Planting partners** *Nicotiana affinis* with *Delphinium*; green nicotiana with *Oenothera biennis* and *Phalaris arundinacea* var. *picta*.

Oenothera biennis
(Evening primrose)

A prolific self-seeder, evening primrose looks good when allowed to wander through a cottage border among other tall plants, especially in a colour scheme based on yellow and purple-mauve. The yellow flowers open up best in the evening, when you also notice their lovely scent. Biennial plants, they are best self-sown.

Size H: 90cm/3ft; S: 45cm/1½ft. **Aspect** Sun. **Hardiness** Hardy. **Soil** Any. **Planting partners** *Lilium*, *Malva*, *Verbascum bombyciferum*.

Pelargonium

This is the cottage window sill plant above all others: go to a pelargonium specialist and buy good old-fashioned named forms instead of modern seed-raised kinds which I consider inferior. Look out for cultivars with variegated leaves, such as 'Mr Henry Cox' (red, green and gold, with single salmon flowers), 'Freak of Nature' (frilly-edged cream leaves bordered with green) and 'A Happy Thought' (spinach-green leaves with a gold-cream butterfly mark in the centre, red single flowers). Cultivars with good flowers include 'Mrs Cannell', a very old salmon-pink single; 'Feuerriese', with huge red pansy like flowers; 'Vera Dillon', with single magenta flowers with a red blotch in the centre; and 'Mr Wren', with single red flowers with a white edge. Root cuttings in peat and sand any time from late spring to early autumn. Old-fashioned pelargoniums are fussy and will need to be grown on in clay pots of soil-based compost. Only try them outdoors in a warm, sheltered spot.

Size H: 30–60cm/1–2ft; S: 30cm/1ft. **Aspect** Sun. **Hardiness** Not hardy. **Soil** Soil-based compost. **Planting partners** Trailing lobelia in tubs.

Salvia

Although the vivid red bedding plants are not cottagey, there are some very attractive and appropriate species valuable for their interestingly shaped late summer and early autumn flowers. *Salvia sclarea turkestanica* has 90cm (3ft) stems of pink, cream and mauvish bracts with tiny blue and white flowers

Oenothera biennis

between them in late summer. *S. farinacea* 'Victoria' has 45cm (1½ft) upright spikes of deep lavender blue; and *S. patens* has extraordinarily striking large, claw-shaped, azure-blue flowers on 45cm (1½ft) bushy growth. (This is actually a half hardy perennial, and can either be brought in for the winter or have its root stored like a dahlia and replanted.)

Size H: 45–90cm/1½–3ft. **Aspect** Reasonably sunny. **Hardiness** Not hardy. **Soil** Any good, fertile, reasonably moisture-retentive. **Planting partners** Each other, *Geranium* 'Anne Folkard', *Sedum spectabile*.

Sweet pea see *Lathyrus odoratus*

Tobacco plant see *Nicotiana*

Wallflower see *Cheiranthus cheiri*

Trees, shrubs and climbers

Buxus sempervirens
(Box)

Box is extremely useful all round the garden. For topiary or an ornamental hedge, it can be clipped into battlements or, more adventurously still, into a rolling, rollicking informal shape to look as though it had been formed by the wind. The dwarf variety, *Buxus sempervirens* 'Suffruticosa', is good for low edgings in a herb garden or round a formal flower bed.

Size Dwarf box can be clipped to H: 15cm/6in; S: 8cm/3in; normal box to H: 60cm/2ft; S: 20cm/8in. **Aspect** Needs at least two hours direct sun per day. **Hardiness** Needs shelter. **Soil** Well-drained, preferably chalky. **Planting partners** Any.

Rosa rugosa 'Fru Dagmar Hastrup'

Chaenomeles speciosa
(Japonica)

Japonica was traditionally grown against the walls of old cottages. Large red, orangey, pink or white chalice-shaped flowers show up against bare twiggy stems in spring, and these are followed by knobbly-looking fruit in late summer and autumn.

Size H: 1.2–1.5m/4–5ft; S: 1.8m/6ft. **Aspect** Sun. **Hardiness** Hardy. **Soil** Well-drained. **Planting partners** Grow clumps of small spring flowers, such as grape hyacinths, underneath.

Clematis

Although not authentic old-fashioned cottage garden plants, clematis have nevertheless found themselves a permanent place in many cottage gardens. Grow them up through ornamental trees and unproductive old fruit trees, or among other climbers over an arch, fence or wall, or allow them to ramble among shrubs as a wild-looking ground cover. Plant clematis in a spot where their roots are shaded by surrounding plants but their tops can grow into sun. Mulch heavily in spring to help them retain moisture. They need plenty of potash during the growing season; I feed mine with liquid tomato feed every two to three weeks, although you could sprinkle a handful of sulphate of potash around each plant in spring, then liquid feed every two weeks with any general purpose liquid feed. Pruning varies: cultivars fall roughly into three groups; the first, which includes 'Barbara Jackman', 'Doctor Ruppel' and 'Nelly Moser', requiring no pruning; the second, which includes 'Comtesse de Bouchaud', 'Etoile Violette' and 'Gipsy Queen', requiring hard pruning (to about 15cm/6in above the ground in early spring); and the third, which includes 'Marie Boisselot', *C. orientalis* and *C. viticella* and their cultivars, being optional. To avoid errors, copy the name and pruning instructions (these should come with the plant when you buy it) on to a plant label and tie this to a strong shoot just above ground level so that you can refer to it as necessary. All clematis should be cut back hard the spring after planting to encourage branching from the base, unless they are already doing so.

Size H and S: Varies according to cultivar. **Aspect** Roots in shade, shoots in sun for at least half the day. **Hardiness** Hardy. **Soil** Chalky to neutral. **Planting partners** Climbing roses, fruit trees.

Elder see *Sambucus*

Honeysuckle see *Lonicera*

Japonica see *Chaenomeles speciosa*

Lonicera
(Honeysuckle)

Cottage garden honeysuckles are self-twining climbers, mostly with scented flowers in summer, good for scrambling up through trees and over arches or rustic poles above a seat. Grow early and late dutch honeysuckles (*Lonicera periclymenum* 'Belgica' and 'Serotina') together so that their flowering seasons

overlap and give continuous purplish-red flowers from late spring to mid-autumn, or for the best scent choose the native woodbine (*L. periclymenum*), with purple-tinged cream flowers from early summer to early autumn: this honeysuckle has been associated with cottage gardens for centuries.
Size H: 6–9m/20–30ft; S: 1.5m/5ft. **Aspect** Sun or shade. **Hardiness** Hardy. **Soil** Any. **Planting partners** *Clematis*.

Myrtus communis
(Myrtle)

This evergreen shrub has large cream flowers with clusters of long stems in the centre in summer. Myrtle is not very hardy and thrives better in an overcrowded cottage garden where it gets plenty of protection from surrounding plants. It also makes a good specimen for growing in a pot by the front door; it can then be moved to a more sheltered situation in winter.
Size H: to 3m (10ft); S: 2.5m/8ft. Normally kept smaller by pruning to remove winter die-back. Stays much smaller if grown in a pot. **Aspect** Sunny. **Hardiness** Needs shelter. **Soil** Well-drained; good in coastal locations and on chalk. **Planting partners** Use as a background to a mixture of cottage flowers.

Rosa
(Rose)

Hybrid Tea roses, never changing from early summer to mid-autumn, look wrong in cottage gardens; old-fashioned roses have more character,

but most only flower for four to six weeks in early mid-summer. Plant them with lots of other cottage garden plants, chosen to flower when the roses are not in bloom. Old-fashioned roses are pruned only to keep them tidy, and many have weak stems that need some support, but they are well worth the effort. A few of my favourites among many are *Rosa gallica* 'Versicolor', syn. *R. mundi* (with red-and-white striped flowers), 'Great Maiden's Blush' (pale pink and very highly scented), 'William Lobb' (a moss rose which changes colour from red through pink then mauve to grey as the flowers fade), 'Chapeau de Napoléon' (with bright pink crested flowers that look like cocked hats), and 'Cardinal de Richelieu' (dusky purple). Species roses such as *R. rugosa* make good cottage hedges.
Size H: 90–150cm/3–5ft; S: 60–120cm/2–4ft depending on cultivar. **Aspect** Sun. **Hardiness** Hardy. **Soil** On the heavy side but not too wet in winter, rich. **Planting partners** *Astrantia major*, bearded irises, *Geranium*, *Lavatera arborea*, *Penstemon*, shrubby salvias.

Sambucus
(Elder)

These are available in several ornamental versions besides the wild elder, which itself looks good growing up through a country hedge or as a specimen tree in a wildish part of the garden. Choose *Sambucus racemosa* 'Plumosa Aurea' for its feathery, cut-leaved, gold foliage and red berries, or *S. nigra* 'Purpurea' for its near-black leaves and palest pink flowers; grow

Lonicera periclymenum 'Serotina'

Trees, shrubs and climbers form part of the permanent framework of a cottage garden, though – with the exception of old-fashioned roses and clematis – most need to be used sparingly for an authentic look.

both as bushes. Elders flower in early summer, followed by summer berries which attract birds.
Size H and S: can reach 3m/10ft but usually kept pruned. **Aspect** Sun; ornamental cultivars like some shelter. **Hardiness** Very hardy. **Soil** Not fussy but prefers chalky soil and tolerates dry conditions. **Planting partners** *Foeniculum vulgare purpureum* and *Lythrum* (cultivated forms of purple loosestrife) with golden elder; *Rosa rugosa* cultivars and *Symphytum × uplandicum* with black elder.

Bulbs and tubers

Spring is the second most important time in the cottage garden calendar, so you need lots of bulbs to create an effective display. Go for species that can be left undisturbed for many years such as narcissi to underplant cottage borders, and keep choicer kinds, like tulips that need to be lifted for the summer, where they can be retrieved easily.

Lilium candidum

Crown imperial
see *Fritillaria imperialis*

Daffodil see *Narcissus*

Dahlia

Dahlias may have fallen from fashion while subdued pastel shades have been in vogue, but they have never been out of favour in tiny working cottage gardens – you still see vivid front gardens full of them in autumn, and they are due for a revival. Plant a dahlia walk (a double border either side of a path) or simply make a dahlia bed to provide an autumn spectacle; use a mixture of dahlias in all colours and sizes, from the biggest spiky flowers to tiny miniature pompons.

Size H: 75cm/2½ft; S: 45–90cm/ 1½ft–3ft. **Aspect** Sunny. **Hardiness** Not hardy; lift and store tubers in a frost-free shed for winter. **Soil** Rich, moisture-retentive but reasonably well-drained, with lots of organic matter. **Planting partners** Each other.

Fritillaria imperialis

(Crown imperial)

Old photographs of cottage gardens, show crown imperials growing in rows among a sea of ground cover plants, or along the edge of a path. They need rich, well-drained soil. Dig in plenty of old manure and a handful of bonemeal before planting (15cm/6in deep in autumn), and sit each bulb on its side on a bed of gritty sand. They bear their showy blooms in spring; most have tawny orange flowers though yellow and double-flowered cultivars can be found. When they become overcrowded, dig up and divide large clumps as soon as the foliage dies down in summer.

Size H: 90cm/3ft; S: 30cm/1ft. **Aspect** Sun. **Hardiness** Very hardy. **Soil** Well-drained, rich. **Planting partners** Late daffodils, *Pulmonaria*.

Lilium

(Lily)

Authentic cottage garden lilies are the madonna lily (*Lilium candidum*), tiger lily (*L. tigrinum*) and turk's cap lily (*L. martagon*). Plant madonna lily bulbs with the noses just showing above ground, in any well-drained soil in sun. Plant tiger and turk's cap lilies in sun or partial shade, 10–15cm (4–6in) deep; the turk's cap is lime-tolerant, but the tiger is not. Other lily species and hybrids all vary in their growing requirements, so check with a bulb catalogue when buying them to see if they suit your soil and situation. In my garden, on clay, lilies rot if left in the soil, so I grow them in large pots plunged in the ground and bring them into a cold greenhouse in winter – this also makes it easy to give lime-free soil to varieties that need it. Some lilies are beautifully scented, especially *L. regale*, *L. × testaceum*, and *L. auratum*. In full shade, grow *L.* 'Mabel Violet', a lovely scented lily with smoky purple flowers. Feed lilies heavily and top-dress them with moist peat or cocoa shell in spring.

Size H: 90–120cm/3–4ft; S: 30cm/ 1ft. **Aspect** Sun or part-shade, depending on species. **Hardiness**

Fruit and herbs

Hardy. **Soil** Rich, well-drained. **Planting partners** *Campanula*, *Clematis*, roses, shrubby salvias.

Narcissus
(Daffodil)

For a cottagey effect, plant daffodils thickly to cover a bank, naturalize them in parts of the lawn and underneath trees, or make clumps in a spring border. Avoid carpet-naturalizing daffodils in a summer border as they have large, long-lasting foliage that persists till mid-summer and swamps anything else you might want to grow in the same spot. Plant clumps towards the back of a border, with perennials in front to hide the foliage after flowering. Daffodils do well in quite heavy soil even if it is wet in winter, so long as it is fairly dry in summer. Avoid dead-heading species naturalized in grass – they self-seed and build up big colonies. Leave naturalized daffodils undisturbed until clumps are overcrowded and not flowering well, then lift and replant the bulbs when the foliage dies down. Good authentic cottage garden cultivars include the pheasant's-eye narcissus (*Narcissus poeticus recurvus*) and its double form, which is very late flowering, the tenby daffodil (*N. pseudonarcissus obvallaris*) and the lent lily or wild daffodil (*N. pseudonarcissus*).
Size H: 30cm/1ft; S: 8cm/3in. **Aspect** Sun to light dappled shade. **Hardiness** Very hardy. **Soil** Fairly heavy, dry in summer. **Planting partners** *Euphorbia*, green-flowered hellebores, or spring flowering shrubs and *Cheiranthus cheiri*.

Fruit bushes

Fruit bushes are essential cottage garden plants: a well-stocked fruit cage is attractive in the same way as a tidy vegetable plot. But if you do not have room, try berries on a wall or fence, or over an arch. Give fruit bushes good, deep, fertile soil which does not lie wet in winter, and a sunny situation; feed in spring and summer with general purpose fertilizer watered in, and bonemeal in autumn; mulch heavily to keep the roots moist in summer. Cover with nets as soon as the fruit forms.
Size H: 1m/3ft 3in; S: 75cm/2½ft. **Aspect** Sun. **Hardiness** Very hardy. **Soil** Good. **Planting partners** Underplant with alpine strawberries.

Fruit trees

Fruit trees are also essential to an authentic cottage garden and a gnarled old apple tree is highly desirable. Fruit trees are available nowadays on dwarfing and semi-dwarfing rootstocks, so it is not difficult to find one to fit even a small garden. Give fruit trees the same soil, situation and feeding as bushes.

Herbs

In cottage gardens herbs can be grown among flowers, for which their foliage provides a good background, or in separate herb gardens. These can easily look very green, so it is worth including good flowering kinds like lavender, thymes, bergamot, clove pinks, evening primrose and nasturtium and coloured-leaved or variegated plants like gilded rosemary, golden marjoram, purple and tricolour

Bergamot
(Monarda didyma)

Fruit trees and herbs, along with vegetables, are probably the oldest authentic cottage garden plants.

sage, purple basil 'Dark Opal', variegated comfrey (*Symphytum grandiflorum* 'Variegatum'), curry plant (*Helichrysum italicum*, with silver leaves), *Pulmonaria* and ginger mint. Good herbs for scent include eau-de-cologne mint, scented-leaved pelargoniums and pineapple sage (*Salvia rutilans*). Include evergreen herbs such as rosemary, bay, and edgings of dwarf box, lavender or *Santolina* to give the herb garden shape in winter.
Size H and S: Varies with species. **Aspect** Sun, sheltered. **Hardiness** Depends on species; some are tender. **Soil** Well-drained. **Planting partners** Box, topiary trees.

Index

Page numbers in *italics* refer to illustrations; numbers in **bold** to the chapter on Key Plants.

Acknowledgments

The publisher thanks the following photographers and organizations for their kind permission to reproduce the photographs in this book:

1 Noel Kavanagh; 2 Clive Nichols; 3 Clive Nichols; 4–5 John Glover; 6–7 Christopher Wood Gallery/Bridgeman Art Library; 8 Tessa Traeger; 9 British Museum/Bridgeman Art Library; 10 The Royal Horticultural Society; 11 Fine Art Photographic; 12 Don Carr/National Trust Photographic Library; 13 left Jerry Harpur (designer Peter Place, Boxford); 13 right Nick Meers; 14 Clay Perry/Garden Picture Library; 16 Jerry Harpur (Mill Cottage, Hitcham); 17 above Jerry Harpur (designer Christopher Grey-Wilson); 17 below Boys Syndication; 18 Jerry Harpur (Chiffchaffs, Chaffeymoor, Dorset); 19 above John Glover; 19 below S & O Mathews; 20 Eric Crichton; 21 Jerry Harpur (Eastgrove Cottage Garden, Sankyns Green, Worcs.); 22 John Glover; 23 above Jerry Harpur (Heide Garden, Melbourne); 23 below Noel Kavanagh; 24 John Glover; 25 Noel Kavanagh; 26 John Glover/Garden Picture Library; 27 National Trust Photographic Library; 29 Eric Crichton; 30 Derek Gould; 31 left Brian Carter/Garden Picture Library; 31 right Brian Carter/Garden Picture Library; 32 S & O Mathews; 33 above Eric Crichton; 33 below Boys Syndication; 34 John Glover; 37 Christine Ternynck; 38 Lamontagne; 40 A-Z Botanical Collection; 41 Jacqui Hurst/Boys Syndication; 45 Steven Wooster/Garden Picture Library; 46 Boys Syndication; 47 Harry Smith Horticultural Collection; 48 John Glover; 49 Clive Nichols; 50 Derek Gould; 52 Marianne Majerus; 53 Brigitte Thomas; 54 Andrew Lawson; 55 left Noel Kavanagh; 55 right Photos Horticultural; 56 Andrew Lawson; 57 Jacqui Hurst/Boys Syndication; 60 Clive Nichols; 61 Clive Nichols; 64 Clive Nichols; 65 Jerry Harpur (designer Penny Crawshaw); 66 Jerry Harpur (designer Michael Balston, Patney, Wilts.); 67 S & O Mathews; 70 Brigitte Thomas; 74 Brigitte Thomas; 77 Didier Willery/Garden Picture Library; 78 Elizabeth Whiting and Associates; 79 Gary Rogers/Garden Picture Library; 80 Eric Crichton; 83 Andrew Lawson; 85 Photos Horticultural; 89 Marianne Majerus; 90 Brian Carter/Garden Picture Library; 91 above John Glover; 91 below Photos Horticultural; 92 Sophie Hughes/NCCPG Collection; 93 David Askham/Garden Picture Library; 96 Michael Perry/Bosvigo Plants; 97 Brian Carter/Garden Picture Library; 98 Marijke Heuff/Garden Picture Library; 99 Andrew N. Gagg; 102–3 John Glover; 104 Marianne Majerus; 105 Christian Sarramon; 106 J.S. Sira/Garden Picture Library; 107 John Glover/Garden Picture Library; 108–9 Hugh Palmer; 110 A-Z Botanical Collection; 112 A-Z Botanical Collection; 113 John Glover; 114 Clive Nichols; 115 Brigitte Thomas/Garden Picture Library; 118 Didier Willery/Garden Picture Library; 119 A-Z Botanical Collection; 120 John Glover; 122 Andrew Lawson.

The publisher also thanks: Carole McGlynn, Barbara Mellor, Barbara Nash and Janet Smy, Michael Shoebridge, Vanessa Luff, and Derek and Judy Tolman.